Pioneering Essays On AI And Law

Advanced Series On Artificial Intelligence (AI) And Law

Dr. Lance B. Eliot, MBA, PhD

Disclaimer: This book is presented solely for educational and entertainment purposes. The author and publisher are not offering it as legal, accounting, or other professional services advice. The author and publisher make no representations or warranties of any kind and assume no liabilities of any kind with respect to the accuracy or completeness of the contents and specifically disclaim any implied warranties of merchantability or fitness of use for a particular purpose. Neither the author nor the publisher shall be held liable or responsible to any person or entity with respect to any loss or incidental or consequential damages caused, or alleged to have been caused, directly or indirectly, by the information or programs contained herein. Every company is different and the advice and strategies contained herein may not be suitable for your situation.

 First Edition.

ISBN: 978-1-95-738602-7

DEDICATION

To my incredible daughter, Lauren, and my incredible son, Michael.

Forest fortuna adiuvat (from the Latin; good fortune favors the brave).

CONTENTS

Note: Visuals are collected together in Appendix B, rather than being interjected into the chapter contents, for ease of reading, enhanced flow, and to see the visuals altogether.

ACKNOWLEDGMENTS

I have been the beneficiary of advice and counsel by many friends, colleagues, family, investors, and many others. I want to thank everyone that has aided me throughout my career. I write from the heart and the head, having experienced first-hand what it means to have others around you that support you during the good times and the tough times.

To renowned scholar and colleague, Dr. Warren Bennis, I offer my deepest thanks and appreciation, especially for his calm and insightful wisdom and support.

To billionaire and university trustee, Mark Stevens and his generous efforts toward funding and supporting the Stevens Center for Innovation.

To Peter Drucker, William Wang, Aaron Levie, Peter Kim, Jon Kraft, Cindy Crawford, Jenny Ming, Steve Milligan, Chis Underwood, Frank Gehry, Buzz Aldrin, Steve Forbes, Bill Thompson, Dave Dillon, Alan Fuerstman, Larry Ellison, Jim Sinegal, John Sperling, Mark Stevenson, Anand Nallathambi, Thomas Barrack, Jr., and many other innovators and leaders that I have met and gained mightily from doing so.

Thanks to Ed Trainor, Kevin Anderson, James Hickey, Wendell Jones, Ken Harris, DuWayne Peterson, Mike Brown, Jim Thornton, Abhi Beniwal, Al Biland, John Nomura, Eliot Weinman, John Desmond, and many others for their unwavering support during my career.

Thanks goes to the Stanford University CodeX Center for Legal Informatics and the Stanford University Computer Science department for their generous support, and for the insightfual and inspirational discussions and feedback from my many fellow colleagues there.

And most of all thanks as always to Lauren and Michael, for their ongoing support and for having seen me writing and heard much of this material during the many months involved in writing it. To their patience and willingness to listen.

CHAPTER 1
INTRODUCTION TO AI AND LAW

This book provides a series of crucial essays encompassing the burgeoning field of AI and the law.

These essays are ostensibly standalone and do not require any prior familiarity with the AI and law topic. You are welcome to read the essays in whichever order you might prefer. The essays have been numbered and sequenced as chapters for ease of referring to the discussions and not due to any need to read one before another.

The essays provide a helpful overview and entry point into the field of AI and law. You will find the essays relatively easy to read and eschew arcane techno-terminology, aiming to layout the vital aspects in clear language and seeking to be readily grasped. The chosen topics entail the latest and hottest trends in the AI and law arena.

For those of you that are potentially interested in knowing more about AI and the law in a deeper way, you might consider my two other books on this subject:

- *"AI and Legal Reasoning Essentials"* by Dr. Lance Eliot
- *"Artificial Intelligence and LegalTech Essentials"* by Dr. Lance Eliot

Those are more akin to textbook-style orientations to the AI and the law field. Both books are available on Amazon and at major bookseller sites. The first book listed provides a comprehensive and detailed exploration of AI and law, while the second book tends to focus primarily on LegalTech and the blending of AI.

One of the most frequent questions that I get asked during my webinars, seminars, and college courses about AI and the law consists of what the phrase "AI and the law" actually refers to.

That's a fair question and deserves a useful answer. In a moment, I will borrow from my other books to provide an explanation about the meaning of "AI and the law" and then dovetail into a brief indication about each of the essays contained in this collection.

Per the essays, you'll end up seeing that there is a great deal of enthusiastic spirit for AI and the law, and likewise a sizable dollop of angst and trepidation about the intertwining of the two. In my view, whether you love it or hate it, there is no stopping the steamroller moving ahead that is going to infuse AI together with the law.

I would urge that any lawyer worth their salt ought to be learning about AI and the law. This will assuredly be especially important for those that are just now starting their legal careers, which I mention because the odds are that the convergence of AI and the law will have an especially pronounced effect throughout your lifelong legal efforts.

For those of you that might be going a more so academic route in the legal realm, rather than being a practitioner of the law per se, the beauty of AI and the law is that there is ample room for new research and a grand opportunity to make a demonstrative mark on the field.

Despite the fact that the field of AI and the law has been studied for many years, dating back to the beginning of the AI field itself, please be aware that we have only scratched the surface on this interweaving. Anyone with a desire to push the boundaries of these two realms will readily find plenty of rampways to do so.

If you are curious about the possible research avenues to pursue, make sure to take a look at my book on *AI and Legal Reasoning Essentials* since it provides a solid foundation on the research to-date and postulates what might be coming down the pike in future research activities. I bid you welcome to the field and wish you the best of luck in your endeavors.

AI And Law

In my viewpoint, Artificial Intelligence (AI) and the field of law are synergistic partners. The intertwining of AI and Law can generally be categorized into two major approaches:

- **AI as applied to Law**
- **Law as applied to AI**

Let us consider each of those two approaches.

AI As Applied To Law

AI as applied to law consists of trying to utilize AI technologies and AI techniques for the embodiment of law, potentially being able to perform legal tasks and undertake legal reasoning associated with the practice of law. Those scholars, experts, and practitioners that have this focus are using AI to aid or integrate artificial intelligence into how humans practice law, either augmenting lawyers and other legal professionals or possibly replacing them in the performance of various legal tasks.

Crafting such AI is especially hard to accomplish, problematic in many ways, and there have been and continue to emerge a myriad of attempts to achieve this difficult goal or aspiration. The rise of LegalTech and LawTech, which is modern digital technology used to support and enable lawyers, law offices, and the like throughout the practice of law are gradually and inexorably being bolstered by the addition of AI capabilities.

There are many indications already of this trend rapidly expanding in the existing and growing LegalTech and LawTech marketplace. Notably, the potent AI and LegalTech/LawTech combination has been drawing the rapt attention of Venture Capitalists (VCs). According to figures by the National Venture Capital Association (NVCA), the last several years have witnessed VC's making key investments of over one billion dollars towards law-related tech startups, many of which have some form of an AI capability involved.

Most of the AI developed so far for LegalTech and LawTech is only able to assist lawyers and legal professions in rather modest and simplistic ways. For example, AI might speed-up the search for documents during e-discovery or might enhance the preparation of a contract by identifying pertinent contractual language from a corpus of prior contracts.

Where the field of applying AI to law is seeking to head involves having AI that can perform legal minded tasks that human lawyers and other legal professionals perform. In essence, creating AI systems that can undertake legal reasoning. This is commonly referred to as AI for Legal Reasoning (AILR).

In a sense, legal reasoning goes to the core of performing legal tasks and is considered the ultimate pinnacle as it were for the efforts to try and apply AI to law. It is undoubtedly one of the most exciting areas of the AI-applied-to-law arena and one that holds both tremendous promise and perhaps some angst and possible somber qualms.

Law As Applied To AI

The other major approach that combines AI and law focuses on the law as applied AI. This is an equally crucial perspective on the AI and law topic.

Sometimes this is also referred to as the **Governance of AI**, though there are those that believe that to be a somewhat narrower perspective on the topic. In any case, the focus is primarily on the governance of AI and how our laws might need to be revised, updated, or revamped in light of AI systems.

You likely already know that AI is experiencing quite a resurgence and has become a key focus of the tech field, along with gaining attention throughout society. AI is being rapidly infused into a wide variety of industries and domain specialties, including AI in the financial sector, AI in the medical domain, and so on.

This rapid pace of AI adoption has opened the eyes of society about the benefits of AI but also has gradually brought to the forefront many of the costs or negative aspects that AI can bring forth. Some assert that our existing laws are insufficient to cope with the advances that AI is producing.

Thus, the need to closely examine our existing laws and possibly revamp them for an era and future of ubiquitous AI.

Expected Impacts

Let's consider how AI and the law can impact those in the AI field, and also contemplate how it can impact those in the field of law.

If you are an AI specialist, you should certainly be interested in the AI and law topic, either due to the possibilities of advancing AI by discovering how to leverage AI into the legal domain or due to the potential of how existing and future laws are going to impact the exploration and fielding of AI systems.

If you are a lawyer or legal specialist, you ought to be interested in the AI and law topic too, for the same reasons as the AI specialist, though perhaps with some added stake in the game.

What is the added stake?

If AI can ultimately become advanced enough to practice law, there is concern by some that it could potentially replace the need for human lawyers and other human legal-related law practitioners.

Some liken this to the famous and telling remark about commitment as exhibited via a chicken and a pig. A chicken and a pig are walking along and discussing what they might do together, and the chicken offers that perhaps they ought to open a restaurant that serves ham-n-eggs. Upon a moment of reflection, the pig speaks up and says that if they did so, the chicken would only be involved (making the eggs), while the pig would end-up being fully committed (being the bacon).

In that sense, AI specialists in this topic are involved, while legal specialists and lawyers are committed.

Meanwhile, for those of you squarely in the field of law, lest you think that AI specialists are to be spared the same fate of being overtaken by AI, you will be perhaps surprised to know that there are efforts underway to craft AI that makes AI, such as in the field of Machine Learning (ML), a specialty known as AutoML, which could potentially put human developers of AI out of a job.

What is good for the goose is good for the gander. Or, it might be that what is bad for the goose is equally bad for the gander.

About These Essays

Now that you've gotten an initial synopsis regarding the topic of AI and law, let's take a moment to briefly take a look at the essays assembled for this decisive collection.

Chapter 1 – Introduction To AI And Law

Key briefing points about this chapter:

- This book is a collection of crucial essays about AI and the law
- The essays are provided as numbered chapters (the sequence is not essential)
- AI and the law consist of two key facets
- One facet is AI as applied to the law (a mainstay of this collection)
- The other facet is applying the law to AI (i.e., governance of AI)

Chapter 2 - AI & Law: Order Taking Associates

Key briefing points about this chapter:

- In some law firms, the associates are treated like order takers
- This can be disheartening to the associates and produce high turnover
- Some partners insist that there would be chaos if associates were allowed to wander
- We consider an example as an illustrative way of exploring the role of associates
- Turns out that AI might aid the matter, taking on the order taking tasks

Chapter 3 - AI & Law: Lawyer Conformity

Key briefing points about this chapter:

- An ongoing debate ensues about the degree of conformity amongst lawyers
- The contention is that law school trains attorneys to be conformists
- This conformity is further reinforced upon entering into nearly any law practice
- The worry is that conformity can be stifling and undermine justice
- AI-based legal reasoning systems are potentially in that same boat

Chapter 4 - AI & Law: Law Firm Rankings

Key briefing points about this chapter:

- Lawyers and law firms are annually ranked by the media
- Ranking can make a sizable difference to a law practice
- The factors used for ranking are wide ranging
- Some assert that the use of AI will become a key factor
- Law practices that adopt AI will be ranked highest

Chapter 5 - AI & Law: Pounding The Legal Table

Key briefing points about this chapter:

- A popular aphorism in the legal field entails pounding the table
- When all else fails, you are instructed to essentially pound the table
- This is a longstanding witticism and has numerous variants
- Some might assume that AI-based legal reasoning will do away with pounding
- In the near term, the AI can strengthen and potentially expand the pounding

Chapter 6 - AI & Law: Believing AI Exceptionalism

Key briefing points about this chapter:

- Companies are churning out AI systems at an astonishing rate
- Many do so with an *AI For Good* mantra, believing in AI exceptionalism
- The harsh reality is that there is also *AI For Bad*
- Attorneys should be ready for clients that are caught in the *accomplice liability* ranks
- One key legal argument entails the question of *substantial unoffending purpose*

Chapter 7 - AI & Law: Liquescent Law

Key briefing points about this chapter:

- The practice of law can be said to be stuck-in-the-mud, inflexible, bloated, etc.
- Some are calling for the legal profession to become nimbly liquescent
- In particular, the *Liquid Legal Institute* is a non-profit entity focused on this aspiration
- Part of their vital effort includes an open collaborative Common Legal Platform (CLP)
- The legal profession all-told needs to come together and aid collectively in this goal

Chapter 8 - AI & Law: Precrime Detection

Key briefing points about this chapter:

- Sci-fi movies are handy for revealing subtle considerations about the law
- One somewhat common theme entails Precrime and the ability to see future crimes
- It is easy to be dismissive of such outlandish notions
- Keep in mind though that we already have predictive policing and other akin aspects
- Advances in AI are bound to extend even further this Precrime predictive quandary

Chapter 9 – AI & Law: Digisprudence

Key briefing points about this chapter:

- Law as code is a topic that continues to be growing in influence
- The notion ostensibly is that we ought to convert our laws into program code
- There is an allied topic involving code as law
- Some assume that the two arenas are the same or identical
- A new term "digisprudence" has been introduced about these matters

Chapter 10 - AI & Law: Catala Legal Coding

Key briefing points about this chapter:

- There is an ongoing debate about the law-as-code confabulation
- Some lean toward low-code or no-code options
- Others emphasize the importance of robust programming capabilities
- Catala is a new programming language devised for the law-as-code ambitions
- Features include lambda calculus and correctness to legal specifications

Chapter 11 - AI & Law: Thinking Like A Lawyer

Key briefing points about this chapter:

- What does it mean to think like a lawyer?
- One essential element would be the logic-based role of argumentation
- Another element would be knowledge of the law
- Some falsely though construe this as a kind of simpleton syllogism
- AI legal reasoning systems will need to go far beyond that approach

Chapter 12 - AI & Law: Legal Engineers

Key briefing points about this chapter:

- Hiring for legal engineers remains brisk and the outlook is assuredly sunny
- There is some confusion in the marketplace about the role of a legal engineer
- They blend the combined expertise of software engineering and the legal realm
- A non-profit professional association exists, the American Society of Legal Engineers (ASLE)
- Legal engineers will continue in demand, even in light of no-code and low-code efforts

Chapter 13 – AI & Law: Circular Legal Reasoning

Key briefing points about this chapter:

- A potential logic-based fallacy consists of using circular reasoning for your arguments
- The usual approach consists of stating a premise as a fact that later is also the conclusion
- Of course, that can be a flawed way of trying to prove your case
- Lawyers often fall into this same trap, though others such as Einstein have done so too
- AI-based legal reasoning systems can aid lawyers in coping with circular reasoning

Chapter 14 – AI & Law: Gluing NLP Benchmark

Key briefing points about this chapter:

- The use of AI natural language systems has been popularized via Alexa and Siri
- On an overarching basis, these are called Natural Language Processing (NLP) systems
- A core subtopic or element within NLP is Natural Language Understanding (NLU)
- NLP and NLU have gradually been emerging in the legal domain, sensibly so
- A new benchmark dataset known as LexGLUE will help level the playing field

Chapter 15 - AI & Law: Quantum Computational Law

Key briefing points about this chapter:

- Existing computers generally continue to use the same hardware design as per the 1950s
- A newer approach consists of quantum computing
- We are in the early days of quantum computers and much still needs to be resolved
- Meanwhile, quantum computing is quite handy for computer uses in the law
- The exciting field of quantum computational law is getting increasing traction

Chapter 16 – AI & Law: Computational Legalism

Key briefing points about this chapter:

- The phrase "computational law" is well-established
- A new phrase that entails a subset has been proffered as "computational legalism"
- Qualms about the similar-sounding naming are worth noting
- Meanwhile, the computational legalism precepts are nonetheless worthy too
- Turns out that AI in the law is likely to aid in mitigating some of those precepts

Chapter 17 - AI & Law: AI You Need To Know

Key briefing points about this chapter:

- AI keeps getting a lot of attention and oftentimes is overhyped
- The use of AI is increasingly being applied into the field of law
- You might be curious as to what the field of AI consists of
- A recent report by the European Commission distills down the essence of AI curricula
- Lawyers knowing what the AI curriculum contains will be prepared when it comes to AI uses

Chapter 18 - AI & Law: Sustainable Legal Informatics

Key briefing points about this chapter:

- Everyone seems to continually refer to the bottom-line
- There is also a trend toward considering the triple-bottom-line or TBL
- Another way to refer to the TBL is to speak of sustainability
- When infusing AI into the law, the TBL or sustainability have not been top-of-mind
- The pell-mell rush toward AI in the law decidedly needs sustainability considerations

Chapter 19 - AI & Law: Shortcomings Of The AI Act

Key briefing points about this chapter:

- Regulators have their eye on AI
- Well-documented examples of AI containing inherent biases and inequities have arisen
- The European Commission has floated a draft regulation, the Artificial Intelligence Act (AIA)
- Europe and other countries around the globe are bound to use the AIA as a cornerstone
- Meanwhile, recent evaluations have shown that the AIA draft has some vital flaws

Chapter 20 - AI & Law: Aged Out AI Predictions

Key briefing points about this chapter:

- Lots of pundits make predictions that they never have to own up to
- In the tech field, there have been some predictions that ended up aging poorly
- Since the first days of applying AI to the law, there have been predictions thereof
- It is worthwhile to take stock of those predictions and see the latest status
- We can also consider how those predictions will far further ahead in time

Chapter 21 - AI & Law: Lawyer Reputation

Key briefing points about this chapter:

- We probably can agree that the reputation of a lawyer is vital to their success
- Those that establish outstanding reputations are going to attract clients
- A reputation that stinks is presumably going to repel clients or not attract them
- Some are seeking to use AI to computationally calculate the reputation of human lawyers
- It could be that AI essentially decides whether you get clients or not

Chapter 22 – AI & Law: AI Judging Judges

Key briefing points about this chapter:

- Trial court cases are routinely appealed and then reviewed by appeals level judges
- You rightfully assume that the appeals level judges are humans
- Some believe that we will inevitably have AI that takes on that role
- The AI would be allowed to affirm or remand the case
- Further levels of appeal would consist of human judges (for now)

Chapter 23 - AI & Law: Online AI Law Courses

Key briefing points about this chapter:

- Lawyers, jurists, and other legal professionals need to be familiar with AI and the law
- The AI juggernaut is already amidst the practice of law and will continue to accelerate
- Besides reading about AI and the law, consider attending online sessions
- Berkeley Law AI Institute is a notable multi-day morning series coming up in November
- This is a highly interactive set of lectures and panels bringing you up-to-speed

Chapter 24 - AI & Law: Overfitting Machine Learning

Key briefing points about this chapter:

- The area of *machine learning* is the darling of the AI realm
- Via machine learning capabilities, we've seen a huge expansion in AI-based apps
- This expansion includes AI-infused LegalTech applications
- Note that machine learning is a type of computational pattern matching
- Quite worrisome is that this means that overfitting can occur (buyer beware)

Chapter 25 - AI & Law: Wet And Dry Code

Key briefing points about this article:

- Law as code is today's popular mantra
- Turns out that the law is not quite the same as programming code
- Some like to refer to wet code and dry code in this context
- A natural language contract would be construed as wet code
- While a smart contract is maybe dry code, or wet code, or something in-between

More About This Book

For anyone opting to use this book in a class or course that pertains to these topics, note that Appendix A contains suggestions about how to use the book in a classroom setting.

Furthermore, Appendix B contains a set of slides that depict many of the salient points made throughout the book.

In some of my prior books, I've interspersed the slides into the chapter contents, but feedback by readers has generally been that readers prefer to not have the textual flow become disrupted by the slides, and instead prefer to have the supplemental material assembled altogether into an appendix.

To make sure that you are aware of those added materials, you'll notice that the ending of each chapter provides a quick reminder about the visual depictions that are available in Appendix B.

And so, with this overall orientation to the nature and structure of this book in mind, please proceed to read the essays and learn about the field of AI and law. I'm truly hoping that you'll find the essays mentally engaging and stimulative to the nature of how the law is being practiced and what the future of the law might become.

Note: *For supplemental materials depicting the aspects discussed in this chapter, refer to Appendix B, which contains various augmented diagrams, charts, and additional related facets of relevance.*

CHAPTER 2

AI & LAW: ORDER TAKING ASSOCIATES

Key briefing points about this essay:

- In some law firms, the associates are treated like order takers
- This can be disheartening to the associates and produce high turnover
- Some partners insist that there would be chaos if associates were allowed to wander
- We consider an example as an illustrative way of exploring the role of associates
- Turns out that AI might aid the matter, taking on the order taking tasks

Introduction

Listen to the sounds of ruckus and exuberant cheers.

A joyous moment in the career of a budding lawyer can be landing a job as an associate in a law firm. You get to rub elbows with seasoned partners that know all the ropes of practicing law. If you keep your eyes open and your ears wide, you can garner some keen legal-beagle insights and demonstratively enhance your legal prowess.

The legal oyster is there for your taking, as it were.

But the reality of the legal world is not quite that rosy. Turns out that sometimes an associate is treated in rather unappetizing ways. Some partners look down upon the associates and tower above them as though the associates are mere legal ants. This includes a general disdain for the legal acumen of the associates.

In short, associates are at times treated like order takers.

A partner barks out an order to an associate and expects the order to be fully carried out, doing so summarily and entirely without reservation or complaint. Get this research done about a sticky legal issue and do it now, bellows the pressed-for-time partner.

Don't ask why. Don't try to get fancy. Just go into a heads-down mode, dig into the legal archives, find the appropriate details, and put together a briefing. Then provide the briefing to the partner and step aside. At that point, akin to being a frantic chaser on an ever-moving conveyer belt, start working heads-down on whatever the next request in line consists of.

Some assert that associates frequently find themselves in the boat of having to do all the grunt work and yet not particularly share in the accolades once the case succeeds. It is our guts and their glory, a disgruntled associate might lamentedly utter about partners that treat associates in such a seemingly denigrated manner.

That being said, a counterargument is that some associates are perhaps only capable of taking relatively strict instructions about what to do. Asking an associate to think outside the box or get creative is bound to be problematic. You can end up with associates that are spinning their wheels. On top of that, if you dare to provide latitude to an associate they might veer far beyond the virtues of the case at hand.

Best to keep a tight rein on those associates.

You see, the precious energy and tangy resources of an associate can be poorly spent if not provided with exacting and altogether precise directives (some say). You need to closely shepherd those associates and hope that someday they will blossom.

Of course, the counterargument to that stingy posture is that if the associates are not allowed to flex their wings, you are stinting their careers and the odds are they will try to move on from their legal practice imprisonment anyway.

So, there you have it.

Differing viewpoints on the treatment of associates.

Are they legal toddlers that need careful and constant handholding, akin to a child that if let loose might unknowingly rush across the street and get badly struck? Or are they an untapped resource that is often sadly misapplied and their true value underappreciated and unrealized?

While you contemplate that conundrum, consider the role of creative or innovative thinking when it comes to undertaking the practice of law. It turns out that AI might be a handy tool for aiding lawyers in a myriad of ways, including being able to find creative solutions to vexing legal problems.

Before we get into the AI specifics, let's consider a quick example that might illustrate this quandary about associates and whether they should be a form of human automata that strictly takes orders.

Going Beyond Orders

In a recent research paper suitably entitled "How to Teach Lawyers, Judges, and Law Students Critical Thinking," Edwin S. Fruehwald provides a personal anecdote about his days as an associate. He first clarifies that the case has been masked to assure privacy aspects, and then he sets the stage for us about the general particulars: "This is like a case I had in practice, but I have significantly changed the facts. Babe Aaron won the MVP award in the NL last year. Six years ago, he was a minor league player whose career was going nowhere. At the time, he was approached by the dominant manufacturer of baseballs with a contract to endorse baseballs."

He next digs further into the nuances: "In exchange for the exclusive right to put Babe's name on baseballs for twenty years, Babe would receive $100 and 50 free baseballs. Babe thought this was great so he signed the contract. Apparently, the baseball company had offered similar deals to all minor leaguers who had been drafted in the first twenty rounds."

The legal trouble enters into the picture this way: "Right after he won the MVP, a different manufacturer of baseballs offered Babe an endorsement contract, which paid him $5,000,000 a year for five years. Babe immediately accepted the offer, and the second company started to market baseballs with Babe's endorsement. The first company sued Babe for breach of contract and the second company for intentional interference with contractual relations."

A partner landed the case on behalf of Babe, and the partner instructed Edwin to research contract defenses with a focus on unconscionability. Though Edwin did so, it occurred to Edwin that there might be more angles of attack: "I noticed that an antitrust violation could be a defense to breach of contract. The dominant manufacturer of baseball had attempted to sign up all minor leaguers who had been drafted in the first twenty rounds. I added this defense at the end of the memo to my partner."

Did Edwin as an associate do the right thing, or did he potentially waste time on researching the antitrust issue? The partner had said to focus on unconscionability. Edwin construed that as guidance, but not binding confinement.

In the end, turns out the partner relished the added element. The case was settled out of court.

Here's how AI comes to play.

Advanced AI for legal reasoning is initially being crafted to do precisely whatever a lawyer asks it to undertake.

This is a veritable order taker. Partners can leverage such AI for the order-taking aspects, and consequently shift the role of associates to going beyond order taking, instilling more legally creative skills and perspectives in their associates.

Conclusion

This should be a win-win. Associates get "upgraded" toward leveraging their human mindset, while still getting the job done of the grungy cornerstone work, being ostensibly performed via using the labor-saving AI.

If that seems rather upbeat, a kicker is that someday the AI legal reasoning might be robust enough that neither partners and nor associates are needed at all.

No worries, though, since that's a long time from now.

Note: *For supplemental materials depicting the aspects discussed in this chapter, refer to Appendix B, which contains various augmented diagrams, charts, and additional related facets of relevance*

Conclusion

CHAPTER 3
AI & LAW:
LAWYER CONFORMITY

Key briefing points about this essay:

- An ongoing debate ensues about the degree of conformity amongst lawyers
- The contention is that law school trains attorneys to be conformists
- This conformity is further reinforced upon entering into nearly any law practice
- The worry is that conformity can be stifling and undermine justice
- AI-based legal reasoning systems are potentially in that same boat

Introduction

Some lament that all lawyers think alike.

This seems a bit confusing and overstated.

We presumably want lawyers that are playing the same game and generally adhering to the same rules. The alternative would ostensibly produce chaos. Imagine analogously being in a baseball world series and nobody agreed to how many bases there are, nor how runs are scored, etc. Nutty! There would have to be a sufficient amount of conformity for the participants to know what needs to be done.

In that case, we might rephrase the claim that all lawyers think alike and instead say that lawyers tend to be conformists. Rightfully so. That is how the legal game is played.

Let's ponder this: *Are all lawyers conformists?*

The primary argument that supports the alleged *conformists* labeling would contend that of course lawyers are conformists. It is the very essence of what they do. You see, it all begins in law school and becomes a dominant pattern thereafter. In law school, you are stridently taught what the law purportedly consists of, and are you then sternly graded, assessed, and authoritatively intoned to abide by that ostensibly legal mumbo jumbo brainwashing throughout your illustrious legal career (they say).

And it isn't just a law school phenomenon.

The moment that you step into a law firm as a junior attorney the conformist shackles are quickly made evident to you. Besides being a conformist about the law, you now have a doubleheader of having to be a conformist to the law firm and how it practices law. This is yet more and more conformity being piled upon the initial lofty batch that you gleaned in your newbie legal studies.

Per legal scholar Andrew Perlman in his notable paper entitled "Unethical Obedience By Subordinate Attorneys: Lessons From Social Psychology" (*Suffolk University Law School Research Paper*, May 2008), here's what he suggests happens in most law practices: "The hierarchical structure of lawyering also makes conformity more likely. Studies suggest that strong conformity forces exist even in arbitrarily constructed groups that hold no long-term power to reward conformity or punish dissent. Lawyers, however, work in groups that are not arbitrarily constructed and actually do hold long-term power to reward conformity or punish dissent. Attorneys typically work in settings where other group members, such as senior partners or corporate executives (e.g., in-house counsel jobs), control the professional fates of subordinates, a condition that increases the likelihood of conformity."

This then illuminates an alarming element about this overwhelming tsunami of conformity amongst those in the legal profession. In essence, the concern is that lawyers fall into a rut of not looking for new and innovative ways to understand the law. Worse still, when coming across untoward legal maneuvers or questionable legal shenanigans in a law firm, the weight of conformity can directly or indirectly suppress attempts to counter the matter (especially as those pressures apply to junior attorneys).

Let's look further at the notion of being in a rut.

A now-classic article that was published in the *Journal of the Legal Profession* in 1976 emphasized the angst about lawyers becoming routinized and unwilling or unable to grasp the need for out-of-the-box thinking: "If competent lawyers must be overly careful in expressing ideas and thought processes, a real question arises as to whether the welfare of our system is being enhanced. A great deal of valid change has been nurtured by imaginative nonconformists, and the legal profession has produced its share" (so stated Harry Cohen in his treatise on "Lawyer Certification, Civility, Good Moral Character, and Pressures For Conformity").

Take this all a step further.

If a lawyer wants to be a *non-conformist*, there are undoubtedly and indubitably personal career-oriented penalties to be paid. According to Cohen: "Nonconformist types of lawyers gain, in the main, radical clients or those who cannot employ other lawyers or whom other lawyers do not want to represent. The radical non-conformist, the revolutionary, has always been shunned by society. They pay a dear price for their luxury, for nonconformity is a quality most of us can ill afford."

Without necessarily agreeing to throw in the towel, let's go ahead and stipulate to some substantive degree that lawyers are conformists. Toss into that rubric that lawyers tend to <u>not</u> be non-conformists (this would seem obvious as an ergo logical extension). The conformity eats away at veering into non-conformity.

AI And The Conformity Racquet

You might be surprised to know that this has significant repercussions for AI in the law.

That proclamation probably seems like a non-sequitur that came out of the left field. Allow me a moment to elaborate.

It turns out that AI is gradually becoming a handy tool for aiding lawyers in a myriad of ways, including being able to find viable legal solutions to vexing legal problems.

Much of today's AI-based legal reasoning systems are being crafted via the use of Machine Learning (ML) and Deep Learning (DL). These are computational pattern matching techniques akin to the use of complex statistics and in-depth mathematics. Typically, you feed lots of legal-oriented data into the computer that is using ML/DL and the algorithms try to discover patterns, for which the AI system can then leverage those patterns for performing legal reasoning (though not quite like humans do, so please don't anthropomorphize this).

Here's the rub.

This reliance on prior data tends to produce an AI system that you could construe as being conformist. In essence, whatever worked before will tend to be considered sacrosanct on a go-forward basis by the AI. You can almost declare that such AI is the ultimate of conformity. Any uncovered non-conformity is usually axiomatically discarded, disregarded, or treated as oddball outliers and of little or no consequence.

An end result is that the preponderance of modern-day AI legal reasoning systems of this ilk is ironically akin to those old sci-fi movies that portrayed futuristic robots as being altogether straightjacket in their mannerisms and facilities. I'm referring to the kind of robot that would do precisely what you said, even if you jokingly told the machine to go jump off a cliff.

Conclusion

The answer to this AI-as-conformist is not to somehow swing to the other side of the spectrum and try to program AI legal reasoning that is crazily non-conformist. That is a bridge too far. We need to recognize the value that non-conformity can provide and harness just the right amount, trying to achieve a balance and serve the desire to attain true justice.

One supposes you could say the same thing about human lawyers and the existent forces that drive attorneys toward conformity. Loosen up and let some non-conformity see the light of day.

Admittedly, it is a catchy idea but takes a lot of hard work to make happen in the day-to-day unrelenting and principally conformist-rewarding legal world.

Note: *For supplemental materials depicting the aspects discussed in this chapter, refer to Appendix B, which contains various augmented diagrams, charts, and additional related facets of relevance.*

CHAPTER 4
AI & LAW:
LAW FIRM RANKINGS

Key briefing points about this essay:

- Lawyers and law firms are annually ranked by the media
- Ranking can make a sizable difference to a law practice
- The factors used for ranking are wide ranging
- Some assert that the use of AI will become a key factor
- Law practices that adopt AI will be ranked highest

Introduction

A law practice can be demonstrably aided or terribly undercut based on the industrywide ranking of the practice.

Law firm rankings or *league tables* are generally perceived as a vital indicator of status, achievement, capability, stability, etc., and represent a plethora of characteristics about the presumed overall worthiness of a law practice. Clients seeking legal guidance are influenced by where a potential law firm resides in such lists, aiming to select a law firm based on how highly ranked the practice is. Newly minted graduates of law schools frequently use ranking lists to decide where to best land their starting job as a lawyer. And so on.

There is a wide array of metrics used by the numerous ranking services. Little if any standardization or even concurrence exists regarding which metrics ought to be used.

In some cases, the metrics are ostensibly transparent and consist of strident quantitative measures such as the number of lawyers employed, profit per partner (PPP), revenue per partner (RVP), and other countable elements. For example, the annual *Global Law Firms 200* listing produced by *Law.com* states that they undertake their ranking by collecting stats of "the world's largest firms by revenue, headcount, and profits per equity partner."

There are also less quantitatively buttressed measures that are primarily qualitative in their nature, including the use of client testimonials, opinion surveys, and the like. Rarely though is just a single metric utilized and instead, a broadly based composite is devised. The result tends to produce rankings based on a proprietary and at times byzantine methodology.

For example, the *U.S. News – Best Lawyers* ranking is vaguely described as using an "evaluation process that includes the collection of client and lawyer evaluations, peer review from leading attorneys, and review of additional information provided by law firms as part of the formal submission process."

The popular and somewhat revered *Vault Law 100* rankings indicate that they "compile a list of the most renowned law firms by reviewing the feedback we receive from previous surveys, consulting our previous lists, poring over legal publications, talking to lawyers in the field, and checking out other published rankings. We then asked these top firms to distribute a password-protected online survey to their associates. We collected all the surveys and averaged the score for each firm. The firms were then ranked in order, starting with the highest average prestige score as No. 1 on down to determine the Vault Law 100." Vault indicates overtly that their approach is based on perception per se: "Remember that in the Top 100, Vault is not assessing firms by profit, size, lifestyle, number of deals, or quality of service; we are ranking the most prestigious law firms based on the perceptions of practicing lawyers at peer firms."

All else being equal, the odds are that the ranking approaches will continue somewhat unabated as is and will axiomatically be routinely used to churn out updated sets of rankings year after year like the making of sausage.

The Future Of Law Firm Ranking

That being said, some new methods will start to emerge as shaped around gradually evolving changes in the legal profession, doing so amidst the emergence of more modern-day practices of law.

Consider a novel ranking scheme discussed by researchers Leonardo Ribeiro and Daniel Figueiredo that involved examining the potential of ranking law firms and lawyers via the use of social networks: "In particular, we are interested in using the lawyers' social network to rank lawyers according to their effectiveness in conducting legal cases. Can the network structure alone reveal the most effective and also influential lawyers in the labor court of the state of Rio de Janeiro? To answer this question, we will consider different centrality metrics to construct a relative ranking of the lawyers. We then evaluate these rankings by quantifying the effectiveness of the lawyers in winning legal cases" (published in the *Journal of Brazilian Computer Society*, 2017).

In short, innovative technology such as that used for enabling online social networking has the strong possibility of inexorably opening the door to new ways of calculating rankings. One form of high-tech that similarly could have a demonstrative impact on law firm rankings consists of Artificial Intelligence (AI) and the adoption of AI-based Legal Reasoning (AILR).

AI is gradually becoming a handy tool for aiding lawyers in a myriad of ways, including being able to find viable legal solutions to vexing legal problems.

There are AI-based e-Discovery apps that can rapidly explore legal documents and ferret out crucial legal discoveries for a given court case. There are Natural Language Processing (NLP) front-ends available for lawyers to use when accessing voluminous datasets of prior legal cases. The AI-based NLP can ease the burden on non-tech-oriented attorneys and speed up the effort undertaken to review legal precedents.

The advent of AI in the law and advances in AILR are predicted to have a demonstrative impact on the practice of law. The expectation is that AI will enable faster lawyering, produce more productive lawyering, improve the quality of lawyering, lower the cost of lawyering, and have other similar substantive impacts.

These impacts will in turn have considerable impacts on law firms.

Envision a law firm that is well-armed with appropriate AILR versus a law firm that eschews the use of AI and remains rooted in everyday conventional means of practicing law.

The AI-infused law firm can potentially do as much if not more legal work than the unarmed law firm, at least on a per lawyer basis. In that case, if a metric such as the number of lawyers is used to rank those two firms, the ranking would potentially be misleading and altogether miss the mark because the headcount alone is insufficient as a proper measure. Depending upon the multiplicity factor of AI-using lawyers, the AI embracing law firm could have a lesser number of lawyers and yet be more productive and have greater legal output than the firm that has more lawyers on the payroll.

Law firms and their rankings will inevitably be revamped to reflect the AI-infusion advantages.

Opinion surveys will likely begin to include questions about whether a given law firm is making use of AI.

Clients are bound to express favoritism toward AI-using law practices as the expectation is that the cost of legal services will decrease based on the use of AILR, along with boosting responsiveness and rapidity of proffering legal guidance. Law firms that have dragged their feet on making use of AI are likely to be perceived as stodgy and outdated, dropping down in the rankings accordingly, meanwhile, law practices favoring AI uses will find themselves moving up in the rankings.

Conclusion

Admittedly, we are not yet at a point of AI-based performance and availability in the practice of law that is capable enough and not widespread enough to move the needle. The inclusion of AI into rankings is still early on.

Nonetheless, the future will entail AI as a keystone for performing legal efforts and will ultimately be disruptive to the existing lawyering practices. This disruption will transform the structure and methods of the ranking services to assuredly include AI adoption factors, causing a shake-up in how law firms are stacked and racked in the eyes of the legal community and the general public at large.

Note: *For supplemental materials depicting the aspects discussed in this chapter, refer to Appendix B, which contains various augmented diagrams, charts, and additional related facets of relevance.*

Conclusion

CHAPTER 5
AI & LAW:
POUNDING THE LEGAL TABLE

Key briefing points about this essay:

- A popular aphorism in the legal field entails pounding the table
- When all else fails, you are instructed to essentially pound the table
- This is a longstanding witticism and has numerous variants
- Some might assume that AI-based legal reasoning will do away with pounding
- In the near term, the AI can strengthen and potentially expand the pounding

Introduction

Your case is going badly. It seems that nothing can be done to turn things around. Then, out of the blue, a seasoned colleague gently inquires as to whether you have tried pounding the table. This nugget of advice was not previously on your mind, but you decide to give it a try.

The oft exhorted and longstanding punchline of "pounding the table" is altogether famous and infamous among most attorneys.

You most certainly have heard the popular aphorism or perhaps repeatedly proffered it while in the throes of trying to devise a last-ditch legal strategy for a thorny case. Here is how the poetic-sounding sage wisdom usually goes: *When the facts are on your side, pound the facts. When the law is on your side, pound the law. When neither is on your side, pound the table!*

I believe we can all agree that this witticism postulates a somewhat worst-case scenario that if you cannot argue and successfully win on the facts or the law, your final resort would be to invoke the classic ploy of all-out fire-and-brimstone. By making a spectacle there is a presumed chance of salvaging your weak posture and wooing a jury or jurist into passionately coming over to your side of things. Of course, this is generally frowned upon and indeed attorneys are usually prohibited from trying to pander overtly toward prejudice, passion, or sympathy in making their case to a jury.

That being said, this doesn't especially stop the urge to pound the table, and nor does it preclude entirely the act of pounding the table. You can cleverly maneuver your way into pounding the table and do so under the ostensible guise of legitimately arguing the merits of your position. Heck, if you don't try pounding the table and yet have already seemingly exhausted all other possibilities, one could suppose that you haven't done all that you can reasonably do to avidly pursue your case (albeit, doing so within the proper thresholds of stringent attorney-ethics behavior).

You might be surprised to know that the pounding punchline has lots of variants.

The most common alternative involves referring to hammering the table. This also requires replacing the notion of pounding with the action of hammering as a consistent theme throughout the catchphrase: *When the facts are on your side, hammer the facts. When the law is on your side, hammer the law. When neither is on your side, hammer the table!*

Hammering appears to have dominated the earlier known versions, dating back to at least the 1910s. I would dare say that today the use of this venerated punchline has to invoke pounding and avert entailing hammering. You see, in a modern context, hammering evokes imagery of vicious activity and conjures visions of the attorney wielding a menacing hammer. The pounding usage seems more benign, alluding to using your fist or hand in lieu of a potentially deadly implement.

There are many more twists and turns to the punchline.

For example, in a poem by Carl Sandburg in 1936, he adds that you should also yell like heck (well, actually, a harsher word is used, shall we say he referred to the adobe of evil down beneath the Earth).

This decidedly seems like sound advice. If you strictly interpret pounding as a speechless act, you probably should be saying something in addition to striking on the table (else few will likely comprehend your physical exertions, of which your crude actions might be regrettably misconstrued). We can though likely dispense with the need to explicitly instruct you to yell out since it seems abundantly apparent you ought to be muttering some form of legal mumbo jumbo while doing the pounding.

Indeed, you might avert any pounding at all and exclusively utilize some magical legal words or similar legal incantation that has the same effect as thumping on the table. Pounding in this weathered maxim surely could be interpreted as a metaphor rather than a literal form of action.

A variant that is best entirely avoided in current times has to do with the directiveness of your pounding or hammering. It used to be that the punchline said to hammer the opposing counsel or to "abuse the other attorney" and thus aim your wrath in a quite directed way. This indubitably carries a dangerous tone in today's world: *When the facts are on your side, hammer the facts. When the law is on your side, hammer the law. When neither is on your side, hammer the opposing counsel.*

The suggestion of undertaking a direct attack at another attorney is obviously worrisome and problematic, even if only for purposes of verbalization (i.e., insidious slippery slopes are hidden within).

AI And The Pounding Of Tables

Shifting gears, there is a great deal of anticipation that AI will gradually become a valued tool for lawyering, including being able to find viable legal solutions to vexing legal problems via AI-based legal reasoning systems.

A common misconception about AI in the legal realm is that the use of AI will excise out all manner of emotion, passion, and sentiment that presently occupies the practice of law. With the advent of AI, there goes a presumed keystone that lawyers and lawyering will become strictly logic-based. No more zany outbursts or attempts to use exaggerated exhortations. The law will be cut and dried, for which AI computationally and precisely figures out the relevant legal arguments of consideration in a court case.

Your desperate remedy of pounding or hammering the table has to be tossed out the window. The new line would seem to be: *When the facts are on your side, pound the facts. When the law is on your side, pound the law. When neither is on your side, you'll need to pound sand.*

Pounding sand is a colloquialism meaning to walk away. In this context, presumably meaning give up and likely losing the case. No self-respecting lawyer ever wants to do that. You always cling to the possibility of some ace in the hole.

The good news is that AI will not eviscerate your option to pound the table. For example, the AI could be programmed to purposely derive tangential arguments that appeal to sentimentality. Thus, luckily for you, the table-pounding could be served up on a silver platter. No need for a lawyer to rack their brain to divine a suitable way to perform the needed pounding, just get one from the AI.

Conclusion

This brings us to a final and yet old-time variant of this esteemed quip: *When the facts are against you, bear down on the law. When the law is also against you, talk your way around it.*

AI can help to enact that mystical wisdom, though it could produce a lot more pounding or hammering or talking by a lot more attorneys, and we should mull over seriously whether that's a good thing or a bad thing. Perhaps this gives rise to another famous saying, namely that an ounce of prevention is worth a pounding of cure.

Note: *For supplemental materials depicting the aspects discussed in this chapter, refer to Appendix B, which contains various augmented diagrams, charts, and additional related facets of relevance.*

CHAPTER 6

AI & LAW: BELIEVING AI EXCEPTIONALISM

Key briefing points about this essay:

- Companies are churning out AI systems at an astonishing rate
- Many do so with an *AI For Good* mantra, believing in AI exceptionalism
- The harsh reality is that there is also *AI For Bad*
- Attorneys should be ready for clients that are caught in the *accomplice liability* ranks
- One key legal argument entails the question of *substantial unoffending purpose*

Introduction

Do you have any clients that are producing AI-based systems?

Even if you don't yet have such clients, you might very well find yourself having such a client in the future.

You need to be ready for a potentially acute legal vulnerability that they are ostensibly unknowingly facing.

I say this because it seems like everyone is eager to get onto the AI bandwagon and they are doing so without considering the downstream legal ramifications.

A lot of companies are simply hurriedly developing and releasing AI-based apps into the marketplace, doing so with great haste. It seems as though each day there is some new breathtaking announcement about a wondrous app that leaps tall buildings due to being AI-infused.

Of course, much of this is mere hype.

The reality for most of these apps is that they tangentially utilize some minuscule AI-related components and otherwise have no special AI-stoked powers per se. In any case, companies are eager to leverage the AI moniker as a means of gaining awareness about something that generally would be considered humdrum or decidedly ho-hum.

Splash the AI pixy dust and you suddenly have a big hit on your hands.

Amid this rush toward the use of AI, there has been a strident belief by many that this is an aboveboard approach to try and craft apps that will benefit mankind. Sure, the AI being infused is perhaps meager now, but it will get better and better over time. This is especially viewed as the upbeat basis for using Machine Learning (ML) and Deep Learning (DL), which are computational pattern matching techniques that can potentially "learn" and improve themselves the more that they are put into use.

The mantra of *AI For Good* has arisen during this pell-mell push toward using the latest AI capabilities. Perhaps AI will aid in solving many of the world's problems that have heretofore been intractable. That has spurred some AI developers to craft AI systems as quickly as possible, but for which they then cut corners and often fail to do due diligence before unleashing their latest AI app creation.

In short, there is a mindset of AI exceptionalism that permeates some of the AI developer ranks.

Get AI out the door and you'll cure the ills of society. This is a lofty mission. They might reluctantly admit that at times the AI is somewhat half-baked. The thing is, perfection is the enemy of the good, they vehemently argue, and the globe needs AI right now. Worry about the flaws and troubles later on.

What has gradually emerged is the wretched underbelly of *AI For Good*, namely *AI For Bad.* Think of using AI for all sorts of unsavory purposes, including for criminal acts. If AI is so handy-dandy for doing good things, it likely can be turned in the opposite direction and exploited for doing bad things. In fact, quite really bad things.

Those that are producing these AI systems are inexorably going to encounter rather severe legal consequences for their foul wares. They just don't realize it, as yet (I'll say more about this in a moment).

Invoking The Legal Principle Of Substantial Unoffending Purpose

We can for convenience's sake categorize the design of AI systems into three primary groupings:

(1) AI designed for legal use
(2) AI designed such that it has dual-use (legal and illegal)
(3) AI designed for illegal use

Here's the legal rub underlying the *AI For Good* and the *AI For Bad* conundrum.

Suppose that an AI system is made available in the marketplace and it ends up getting used for criminal acts. You are hired by the developer or the company that produced the AI system. It is your job to aid your client as they seem likely to soon be mired as a defendant in legal proceedings entailing the illegal acts undertaken via their AI system.

If the AI was crafted for legal use but was nonetheless "misapplied" by some user to undertake a dreadful illegal use, what is the criminal liability facing the original AI developer or company that produced the AI system?

Criminal law research by Benton Martin and Jeremiah Newhall note that this is potentially a form of accomplice liability: "This Article focuses on one type of criminal liability—accomplice liability—that can act as a dragnet on providers of technology that lends itself to criminal use. In particular, a violation of the federal statute for aiding and abetting, 18 U.S.C. § 2, can be implied in every charge for a federal substantive offense, and there is a potentially troubling strain of cases holding that knowing assistance can be enough to deem someone an aider and abettor, even without stronger evidence of a shared criminal purpose" (as per *Journal of Criminal Law and Criminology*, Winter 2014, "Technology and the Guilty Mind: When Do Technology Providers Become Criminal Accomplices").

Assume that the AI system your client released was developed with the utmost of altruistic motives and falls into the categories of design for legal use or the design that has dual-use facilities. The third category, AI designed for illegal uses is an obviously less legally arguable posture of wiggling out of.

Your client is under the gloomy cloud of an *accomplice liability* charge. The client will undoubtedly profess their innocence and indignantly declare that AI exceptionalism is their righteous cause. As starkly stated by Martin and Newhall: "Many accused technologists try to exculpate themselves, with mixed success, by claiming ignorance of specific instances of their technology's criminal use."

Can the proverbial head-in-the-sand defense be their savior? The researchers stridently contend this is wholly unlikely: "Technologists cannot sit idly while their technologies find criminal use, as the very act of not intervening pushes them closer to criminal culpability."

A crucial legal concept to keep in mind is the role of *substantial purpose*, consisting of either an unoffending or offending basis. If the AI system truly fits into the category of a design for strictly legal uses, there should be an abundant indication that it was devised with a *substantial unoffending* purpose. Your presumed advisable course would be to bring forth that as a key part of the defense strategy.

The counterargument likely made by the prosecution would be that the unoffending purpose was not substantial and instead was merely marginal or inconsequential. On top of that, the ideal goal of the prosecution would be to successfully argue that the AI system was concocted with a *substantial offending* purpose at its core.

That is the giant steely nail in the coffin undermining your defense.

Conclusion

Let's briefly reconsider the earlier indicated three categories of AI systems. In the real world, few AI systems can reasonably be classified in the category of AI designed for legal use alone. By and large, everyday ordinary AI systems are in the dual-use category.

Please mentally prepare yourself for the seemingly shocking naïve legal viewpoint by AI exceptionalism advocates. They will either be blind to the dual-use adverse aspects of their beloved AI system or try to sidestep the possibility of criminal use by dreamily fantasizing that illegal uses would not ever arise.

You'll need to splash some startlingly cold legal waters on those flag-waving AI-as-liberator devotees.

Note: *For supplemental materials depicting the aspects discussed in this chapter, refer to Appendix B, which contains various augmented diagrams, charts, and additional related facets of relevance.*

CHAPTER 7

AI & LAW: LIQUESCENT LAW

Key briefing points about this essay:

- The practice of law can be said to be stuck-in-the-mud, inflexible, bloated, etc.
- Some are calling for the legal profession to become nimbly liquescent
- In particular, the *Liquid Legal Institute* is a non-profit entity focused on this aspiration
- Part of their vital effort includes an open collaborative Common Legal Platform (CLP)
- The legal profession all-told needs to come together and aid collectively in this goal

Introduction

Let's talk about liquid.

Not just about any kind of liquid. I'm referring specifically to *liquid legal*. That certainly must seem an unusual phrasing, perhaps intriguing to you and not at all the type of catchphrase that you are likely used to seeing in the everyday throes of your law practice.

Allow me a moment to back up and provide a greater context to the matter at hand.

We know that physicists can regale you with all sorts of particulars about the different states of matter. There are as far as we know just four primary observable or so-called natural states, consisting of matter that is either a liquid, a solid, a gas, or plasma.

That of course is the relatively simplified view of things. The reality is that there are other extraordinarily exotic states which are not seemingly naturally occurring but for which we can theorize might exist or that we can actively produce via elaborate and somewhat extreme exertions.

It is generally feasible to also get a given state to transform into one of the other states. In some instances, the transformation is relatively easy to carry out. There are though transformations that are quite arduous to attain. Sometimes an immense amount of high energy is needed to affect the desired transformation.

Why am I dragging you through an introductory treatise on physics and states of matter?

Because of the latest trend toward achieving *liquid legal*, as it were.

An entity known as the *Liquid Legal Institute* has been embarking on a seemingly herculean pursuit of trying to transform the practice of law into becoming nimbly liquescent. Their scope is perhaps even wider than what you might think it is, depending upon your personal definition of the practice of law. The broadest depiction would allude to the entirety of the legal ecosystem.

Returning to the discussion about states of matter, you could construe today's legal efforts as overwhelmingly being mired in something ostensibly characterized as tedious, bloated, stodgy, and adversely overly solidified, maybe even fossilized. There is an overreliance on old-time paperwork type of processes and the practice of law seems regrettably stuck in bygone days.

I'm sure you get my drift.

In short, we need to shift the legal world from being a solid to becoming a liquid.

That is a rather plain-spoken and altogether heralded aspiration. The immense problem is how to get from the existent stuck-in-the-mud solidified state into a modern-day fluidity or liquescent state. A gutsy and earth-shattering amount of energy is likely going to be required to get lawyering into the condition of being summarily agile, seamless, rapid, flexible, and otherwise be as smooth as a velvety fine wine.

Source Of The Liquid Legal Underpinnings

The key genesis and cornerstone foundation for the overarching liquid legal perspective were extensively articulated in an edited collection of papers in 2017 by Kai Jacob, Dierk Schindler, and Roger Strathausen, as published in a notable book entitled "Liquid Legal: Transforming Legal into a Business Savvy, Information Enabled, and Performance Driven Industry."

The core premise underlying the liquid legal mantra is the bold assertion "that the new legal function will shift from a paradigm of security to one of opportunity; that future corporate lawyers will no longer primarily be negotiators, litigators, and administrators, but that instead, they will be coaches, arbiters, and intrapreneurs; that legal knowledge and data-based services will become a commodity; and that analytics and measurement will be key drivers of the future of the profession" (as stated by the book authors).

Momentum toward the liquid legal notion has been mounting and a second book by the same authors was published in 2020 entitled "Liquid Legal: Towards a Common Legal Platform." This additional look at the liquid legal effort provides "an outlook on how legal professionals will operate in the future, but also allows readers to develop a genuine understanding of the value of digitalization, standardization and new methodologies" (as summarized by the authors).

An especially outstanding element of these efforts is the aim toward divining a Common Legal Platform (CLP). The hope would be to produce an open platform that would readily allow a plug-and-play across all kinds of LegalTech that might be devised for the legal ecosystem. I've been a longstanding proponent of seeking open standards in the legal high-tech arena, desiring to avert and inexorably overcome the downsides of incompatible proprietary approaches.

The Liquid Legal Institute is embarking actively on formulating and promulgating a Common Legal Platform. This already has entered into a budding state of reality. You can visit their GitHub site to access the programming code already crafted (note that GitHub is a popular online website service for storing computer programs and potentially doing so on an open-source basis).

As indicated by the Liquid Legal Institute, serving in its capacity as a non-profit entity that considers itself as technology-affine and a strident legal ecosystem open collaborator: "The CLP is intended to serve as a place for co-operation, interaction, and exchange – not only among people but also among IT systems and between people and IT systems. For such co-operation, interaction and exchange in a decentralized network, connecting structural elements and technical standards."

There are four major layers to the architecture, containing a (low-level to high-level) Technology layer, Data layer, Application layer, and Utilization layer. Descriptions, specifications, and related code are in various initial states and incrementally being advanced.

This is all just in its infancy and we'll need to get a lot more parties to partake in these burgeoning transformative activities.

That reminds me of those darned fortunate physicists.

You see, physicists tend to delightedly drool over their nifty and pricey particle physics accelerators such as the massive Large Hadron Collider (LHC) operated by CERN in Geneva, Switzerland. Good for them!

Those lucky and enterprising physicists have the means to explore states of matter and make potentially life-altering discoveries about our existence and our future.

The legal profession needs likewise to galvanize together. Our collective spirit ought to strive toward moving out of a solid-state and into a liquid state. We don't even necessarily need to spend the many billions of dollars that it took to construct the LHC (which, admittedly, did aid in discovering the Higgs boson, so presumably that was money well-spent, one assumes).

For the law and the practice of law, transformation is vital. The aim is to bolster and expand the life-changing need for wider and unimpeded access to justice.

Conclusion

Making such a transformation is going to be hard, no doubt about that. But we at least know where we should be heading. Let's get today's legal rigidity to incrementally melt away and beneficially transform into a preferable liquid-like fluidity state.

I'll drink to that.

Note: *For supplemental materials depicting the aspects discussed in this chapter, refer to Appendix B, which contains various augmented diagrams, charts, and additional related facets of relevance.*

Dr. Lance B. Eliot

CHAPTER 8
AI & LAW: PRECRIME DETECTION

Key briefing points about this essay:

- Sci-fi movies are handy for revealing subtle considerations about the law
- One somewhat common theme entails Precrime and the ability to see future crimes
- It is easy to be dismissive of such outlandish notions
- Keep in mind though that we already have predictive policing and other akin aspects
- Advances in AI are bound to extend even further this Precrime predictive quandary

Introduction

Do you like sci-fi movies?

Some people relish them, while others find them farfetched and lacking in realism. Give me a moment to hopefully prove to you that some sci-fi movies have worthwhile content pertaining to lawyering and provide enriched fodder for contemplating the law and the future of the law.

That's a high bar perhaps to hurdle, but let's try.

We'll start with one of my favorite all-time sci-fi films, *Edge of Tomorrow*, which features the veritable mega-star Tom Cruise in his usual kind of heroic role. He has an especially eye-catching line in that futuristic portrayal, consisting of something like this: *I am going to tell you a story, which at first is going to sound ridiculous, but the longer I talk the more rational it is going to seem.*

I don't want to particularly give away the all-told plot of the film, so I'll merely emphasize that (spoiler alert) the gradually revealed reason that the story being told would appear to be preposterous is due to the outsized claim by Tom Cruise's character that he is able to see the future. Of course, we all know that the future is the future and until time travel is invented there doesn't appear to be any means of knowing what the future holds.

You might be aware of another Tom Cruise movie that also dealt with being able to divine future events, namely the now-classic *Minority Report*. I am pretty sure that you must have heard of this sci-fi movie or possibly seen it, due to the aspect that it has to do with laws and law enforcement.

Again, in my effort to avoid spoiling the film entirely for you if you haven't seen it, allow me to just mention that the plot involves human psychics known as precogs that can see the future encompassing criminal acts. Due to their foreknowledge of especially heinous crimes that are going to be committed in the future, society has established a police department labeled as PreCrime that is utilized to capture those future criminals before they can undertake their monstrous crimes.

I assure you that any lawyer having an inkling of interest in sci-fi has got to watch that movie and will be undoubtedly glad that they did so. Sure, the idea is outstretched and the movie special effects are somewhat outdated (the movie was released in 2002), but as a combined whodunit, murder thriller, and a lot of future-tech wizardries shown, you've got to relish the fascinating take on how laws and law enforcement might someday be altered.

Speaking of which, I'd like to tell you a story about AI and the law.

The story at first is going to seem ridiculous, but the more I unravel the story the more rational it is going to seem.

Precrime And The Detective Role Of AI

Are you ready?

In an engaging research paper entitled "Does 'Precrime' Mesh with the Ideals of U.S. Justice? Implications for the Future of Predictive Policing," authors Jackson Polansky and Henry Fradella at Arizona State University (ASU) tackle the real-world legal possibilities of a *Minority Report* kind of scenario (published in the Cardozo *Public Law, Policy and Ethics Journal*, 2016)

You might immediately scoff at the research worthiness of entertaining the wild and ostensibly crazy propositions underlying Precrime or precogs. Likely, your first thought is bound to be that precogs do not exist today and there is absolutely no viable foundation for believing that precogs are going to ever exist.

As such, you are using impeccable logic to argue that there is no point in considering any semblance of our having grand visions showcasing that a future crime is going to be committed. Simply stated, no one can time travel forward and know what the future is going to be. It seems impossible.

And so, the trap has been set.

We need to shift our gaze away from being able to see the future and instead focus on being able to predict the future.

Here's what the researchers suggest we seriously ponder: "At the outset, we want to make it clear that this paper is premised on the potential evolution—perhaps even the probable evolution—of current predictive policing to a terminus of precrime. Such an outcome may never occur. But given the possibility of harnessing data to predict future crimes, this paper advances arguments about the legal and moral implications of such a scheme, especially in light of the relatively low standards of proof necessary to support a variety of police actions, including reasonable suspicion to stop, question, and perhaps even frisk a suspect, and probable cause to conduct a search, seize evidence, or make an arrest."

In short, the point is that we already have a rather clearly established criminal justice system that to some substantive extent relies upon the prediction of crimes. We use extensive data about crimes committed per geographical area, and link this to property records, consumer financial data, weather information, and the like, using this to try and predict when, where, and what crimes will be likely committed. The authors clarify that this currently is predominantly place-based versus person-based, though person-based is on the rise: "While some forms of person-based predictive policing exist today, person-based predictive policing is far less developed than place-based predictive policing. Yet, it is this latter type of prediction that we anticipate growing in the future since it has already been piloted, in rudimentary forms, in several U.S. cities."

The advent of AI is going to spur those capabilities and assuredly enable stronger and stronger efforts of predicting crime, including place-based and person-based particulars.

Do not though confound this use of AI with some form of machine-based sentience or those fantastical imaginative dreams that AI can divine the future. Nope, that's not in the cards for now.

Instead, the crux is that AI is a handy computational pattern matching tool. The more data there is available, the better off the AI predictive facility is likely to be. We already are awash in data and you can abundantly expect that even more data is daily being surfaced and stored.

Law enforcement will be able to use AI predictive algorithms to try and inch toward the precog knack of foreknowledge.

Conclusion

That being said, we need to take a deep breath and realize that these are merely predictions. They are not the same as "knowing" the future. The law already does allow for preventive detention, and we will certainly be debating the legally permissible and sensible probable cause that AI-based crime prediction brings to the fore.

You can be the judge as to whether AI, as infused into the law, is a friend or foe in these matters, or whether the matter is really contained wholly within the hands of mankind that will ascertain how we use AI for better or for worse.

Note: *For supplemental materials depicting the aspects discussed in this chapter, refer to Appendix B, which contains various augmented diagrams, charts, and additional related facets of relevance.*

CHAPTER 9

AI & LAW: DIGISPRUDENCE

Key briefing points about this essay:

- Law as code is a topic that continues to be growing in influence
- The notion ostensibly is that we ought to convert our laws into program code
- There is an allied topic involving code as law
- Some assume that the two arenas are the same or identical
- A new term "digisprudence" has been introduced about these matters

Introduction

Let's engage in a bit of Algebra 101 and discuss the nature of inverse functions.

Dust off those cobwebs in your mind and hark back to some key mathematical fundamentals that you presumably learned in your basic algebra classes while in college.

An inverse function is a mathematical function that is the reverse of another function. Sometimes also referred to categorically as anti-functions, the input fed into one function produces an output that for which if fed into a second function will produce the same value as the original input that was fed into the first function.

Whoa, that seems a bit dizzying.

Perhaps the straightforward approach is to say that if we have a function A wherein an input of some particular value X gives an output of some particular value Y, the inverse function B could be fed an input of that same Y and produce an output of that same X. Thus, X goes into function A, producing Y. Y can be fed into function B, producing X. There is a one-to-one relationship for each of the respective values of X and of Y.

Imagine that we opt to feed the value of 3 into the function A and the output is 6. The invertible function would be a function B that upon receiving the input value of 6 produces the output value of 3. To strictly be inverse functions, this same invertibility has to exist for the entirety of all values entailing function A and function B.

You'll see in a moment the reason that I am dragging you through this mathematics core dialogue.

We will momentarily shift gears.

Many in the legal profession are touting the idea of law as code. Briefly, the law as code mantra refers to the assertion that the law per se can be considered as a form of programming code. The text of the law is regarded as a set of rules that can be codified into a program or algorithm.

Converting the usual and ordinary text of laws into code would be quite handy since we could then use computers to aid in analyzing and making use of the law. Today's text-based laws are flat and inactive when sitting on the books all by themselves.

They are just blobs of text. If we were to transfer laws into code, the computer could enliven the laws by being able to computationally access them and do logic-based inferences with our laws. This would ostensibly make laws into being active and much more usable and useful.

The use of AI in the law is anticipated to make the law as code a likelier possibility.

Now that we've artfully covered the law as code topic, this might seem vaguely reminiscent to you of another trendy catchphrase, namely code as law.

Code as law is the notion that a given computer program could be said to resemble a set of laws. The code is acting as though it articulates encoded laws-of-the-land. Suppose for example that a computer program was written that embodies the traffic laws in the city that you live in. When a cop issues a ticket, the ticket is entered into the computer program to verify which laws were broken (or indicate that no laws were transgressed). You could earnestly suggest that the code of that program is a surrogate for the traffic laws in that jurisdiction.

Not wanting to blow your mind but envision further that there aren't any preexisting text-based traffic laws in that locality and the only embodiment of the laws is the code of that particular program. This implies that we don't necessarily need to have text-based laws at all. We might instead simply rely upon computer programs as our encoded laws.

Some argue that we ought to be more modern-day about our laws and skip the old-time text, whilst instead jumping directly into using code.

Questioning The Two Assertions

Here's your million-dollar question for the day: *Is code as law a veritable inverse function of law as code?*

Drum roll, please.

The answer is a resounding no.

And that makes for legally troubling qualms.

You see, the code as law might have little or no bearing on the laws as we have enacted them. The code is an interpretation of the law as so interpreted by a programmer, and worse still is the daunting aspect that the code might contain phantom or made-up law that has nothing to do with the laws themselves.

In an interesting legal research paper by Laurence Diver, this point about the downsides or outright dangers of code as law are emphasized: "So whereas text-based legal norms are in a sense passive, lying in wait to be interpreted, complied with, and perhaps enforced or declared null by a court, code simply goes ahead and enforces some configuration of regulative force that might bear no relation whatsoever to either the requirements of substantive law or any other external requirement" (as published in the journal of *Law, Innovation & Technology* in an article entitled "Digisprudence: The Design of Legitimate Code").

The researcher contends that code as law is demonstratively both more and yet simultaneously less than the law: "Code is thus not law; it is instead both more, and less, than law. More, because of the instrumental power of design to constitute and regulate user behavior. But simultaneously less, because it lacks the normative mechanisms that aim to keep its textually-bound sister in check."

This leads those in the law to be forewarned about where the code as law might be heading, per Diver: "It is precisely because code lacks the checks and balances of legality but nevertheless has immense power to shape behavior that it is necessary to instantiate some form of 'constitutional' protection in the materiality of its design."

The author coins a new vocabulary word that he calls *digisprudence*.

This would consist of a legal field that focuses on establishing the legitimacy and illegitimacy of digital artifacts or designs that embody a regulative effect on human behavior. He calls for strident efforts to establish mechanisms of ex-ante legitimation and ex-post remediation for code as law.

Conclusion

I think we can generally agree and perhaps wholeheartedly all concur that we should not allow computer programmers to silently and subtly slink their way into the role of unchecked quasi-legislators that divine what our laws are to be. It is altogether hair-raisingly scary to think of an everyday coder as having quasi-sovereign powers.

Code as law requires a clear-cut need for accountability, contestability, and full-on transparency. Of course, you could make a similar though not identical case for the concerns about law as code too. They are both quasi-legal mathematically oriented functions requiring openness and lawyer-minded scrutiny.

Note: *For supplemental materials depicting the aspects discussed in this chapter, refer to Appendix B, which contains various augmented diagrams, charts, and additional related facets of relevance.*

CHAPTER 10

AI & LAW: CATALA LEGAL CODING

Key briefing points about this essay:

- There is an ongoing debate about the law-as-code confabulation
- Some lean toward low-code or no-code options
- Others emphasize the importance of robust programming capabilities
- Catala is a new programming language devised for the law-as-code ambitions
- Features include lambda calculus and correctness to legal specifications

Introduction

Take a look at just about any legal news media posting these days and you'll inevitably see a reference to the law as code. The assertion that law is code has become nearly ubiquitous.

Why so?

Well, the overarching notion of law as code is that the law can be construed as a form of programming code.

The text of the law is ostensibly regarded as a set of rules that can be summarily codified into a program or algorithm. If that is so, we can readily pour the law into computers and be able to easily access the law more actively.

Rather than ordinarily dealing with inactive blobs of text, a computer system that has ingested law as code would be able to computationally aid lawyering. Logic-based computations could make inferences about our laws, turning the law into something enlivened and usable. Just imagine that instead of trying to do byzantine text searches to figure out the law that pertains to your particular legal case at hand, you could ask the computer to do the legal intertwining for you.

The use of AI in the law is anticipated to make the law as code an even likelier possibility.

With all this excitement about law as code, you might be puzzled as to why we haven't already witnessed gobs of laws being overnight plunked down into computers as code. Presumably, it ought to be easy-peasy to do so. Take any given law, which seemingly is supposed to be "code" that is suitable for computers, dump it into a computer as code, and voila, you have yourself the final result of law as code.

The thing is, the law is not really code per se.

Law as code is an outstretched misnomer that keeps getting repeated, over and over again. You would be better off thinking of the law as something that resembles code. This resemblance fools people into believing that it is merely a quick half-step toward actually being code. Sorry to say that the law and program code are miles apart from each other.

That's a cold hard fact.

A key difference is that the law suffers from semantic non-determinism. In plainer speak, our laws are written in conversational natural languages such as English. As a lawyer, you know how much leeway there is in the interpretation of our laws.

You cannot just isolate a particular sentence in the law and know for sure the precise meaning of that law.

This point is reminiscent of a favored quote that appeared in a California Supreme Court case noting how the law is loosey-goosey interpretable: "Our fundamental task is to determine the Legislature's intent so as to effectuate the law's purpose. We first examine the statutory language, giving it a plain and commonsense meaning. We do not examine that language in isolation, but in the context of the statutory framework as a whole in order to determine its scope and purpose and to harmonize the various parts of the enactment. If the language is clear, courts must generally follow its plain meaning unless a literal interpretation would result in absurd consequences the Legislature did not intend. If the statutory language permits more than one reasonable interpretation, courts may consider other aids, such as the statute's purpose, legislative history, and public policy" (Sierra Club v. Superior Court (County of Orange), 57 Cal.4th 157, 2013).

But that's not all, there is also this additional adage: "Furthermore, we consider portions of a statute in the context of the entire statute and the statutory scheme of which it is a part, giving significance to every word, phrase, sentence, and part of an act in pursuance of the legislative purpose."

When you compare this depiction to the type of code that is used in computers, there is a vast gap between the preciseness expected of programming code and the nebulous mushy semblance of laws cast in everyday English. Transforming the law into suitable equivalent code is a herculean task and one that still defies myriads of serious attempts at resolving.

How To Program Our Way Out

One of the historical and still ongoing approaches consists of devising specialized programming languages that are targeted expressly for representing laws as code. The hope would be to have a coding language that is suitable for lawyers to comprehend and thus participate directly and substantively in the programming efforts.

A research team has crafted a new programming language they call Catala that tries to provide features tuned to the law as code mantra. First, they highlight why such a tool is needed to deal with laws that are text-based prose: "Unfortunately, prose remains a woefully inadequate tool for the job. The lack of formalism leaves room for ambiguities; the structure of legal statutes, with many paragraphs and sub-sections spread across multiple pages, makes it hard to compute the intended outcome of the algorithm underlying a given text; and, as with any other piece of poorly-specified critical software, the use of informal, natural language leaves corner cases unaddressed" (per co-authored article by Denis Merigoux, Nicolas Chataing, and Jonathan Protzenko, entitled "Catala: A Programming Language for the Law" in the Proceedings of ACM Programming Languages, August 2021).

Be aware that seeking to provide a programming language that is equally usable by lawyers and by software engineers is a tough line to hoe. Many such attempts have either steered too far to one side or the other. Worse still, some have ended up in a no man's zone, whereby neither specialty relished the language. The researchers acknowledge this predicament: "Catala aims to bring together lawyers and programmers through a shared medium, which together they can understand, edit and evolve, bridging a gap that too often results in dramatically incorrect implementations of the law."

In their paper, the researchers highlighted the various capabilities of Catala. In addition, an informal usage analysis was done with the aid of eighteen law school graduates in a master's degree program. All told, Catala is an interesting addition to the various law-coding programming languages and time will tell whether it gains traction.

Conclusion

For those of you that are considering the low-code or no-code approach to law as code, you likely would eschew this kind of option. On the other hand, this is a horse race for which we don't know which of the horses is going to yet win. Catala is a full-on coding scheme that proffers robust safeguards for assuring correctness to legal specifications. That's something few of the lighter versions of law as code provide.

Right now, your best bet consists of stridently paying attention to the full range of horses that are in the law-as-code heretofore insurmountable and still quite open-ended race.

Note: *For supplemental materials depicting the aspects discussed in this chapter, refer to Appendix B, which contains various augmented diagrams, charts, and additional related facets of relevance.*

CHAPTER 11
AI & LAW: THINKING LIKE A LAWYER

Key briefing points about this article:

- What does it mean to think like a lawyer?
- One essential element would be the logic-based role of argumentation
- Another element would be knowledge of the law
- Some falsely though construe this as a kind of simpleton syllogism
- AI legal reasoning systems will need to go far beyond that approach

Introduction

Lawyers often chuckle when they hear a comment that a non-lawyer is said to think like a lawyer.

You can become quite self-reflective about what that portends. In some instances, the altogether offhand remark suggests that someone is seemingly thinking in a rather rules-based manner and exhaustively exploring all the angles on a given topic. This ostensibly is a fair or at least sensible comparison to lawyers since the act of lawyering does indeed entail a heavy-duty focus on the rule of law and how to divine a comprehensive and all-sides explored legal argument.

Notice that thinking *like* a lawyer has a somewhat different connotation than referring to actual lawyerly based thinking per se.

Someone that thinks like or is akin to the thinking processes of a lawyer might be contemplating matters that have little if anything to do with the law itself. You could say that a physicist mulling about atomic and subatomic particles was invoking lawyer-like mental exertions, doing so when trying to figure out the myriad of rules that govern nuclear reactions and also assessing which rules seem applicable to a particular fissionable reaction at hand.

A lawyer that does lawyering is presumably the real deal when it comes to thinking like a lawyer.

They are officially a lawyer by way of ascertained certification or licensing, and they are thinking (hopefully) in a manner consistent with the role and expected practices of being an attorney. Of course, not every thought that enters into the noggin of a lawyer is necessarily the thinking of a lawyer since it would seem a bit disingenuous to say that when you are ordering a sandwich for lunch that you are fully functioning in a true lawyering fashion.

Okay, so we have set the stage that the phenomena of thinking as a lawyer is the cornerstone of lawyering and consists of at least two major elements, namely that you are versed in the law and the practice of law, and that you have the mindful acumen underlying aspects such as legal argumentation and the like. The latter element is more so about being trained in and capable of certain ways of logic-based thinking and problem solving, for which those that think like or similar to a lawyer can also share in the same semblance of coherent thinking though applied to other domains outside of the legal domain.

AI And That Thinking Like A Lawyer Conundrum

I've led you up to the doorway of an intriguing dilemma associated with the advent of AI in the practice of law.

First, as background, there are ongoing efforts to craft AI-based legal reasoning systems that can be used in solving legal issues. These AI capabilities are predominantly aimed currently at aiding human lawyers, acting as a helping hand to an attorney facing a challenging legal question.

In the future, some fervently believe that we will be able to achieve autonomous AI legal reasoning that can perform legal tasks on par with human attorneys and ergo not need a human lawyer to be in the loop therein.

One claimed stumbling block for AI being able to break out of the sidekick role and shift into an autonomous mode is that the existent AI legal reasoning systems tend to "think" in a manner unlike the thinking of a lawyer. Allow me to quickly emphasize that there isn't any AI that is sentient and we need to be careful in anthropomorphizing today's AI facilities.

To showcase what is meant by not thinking like a lawyer, we can refer to an enlightening discussion about lawyering in the now-classic article from the *Cornell Law Review* published in 1924 and entitled "Logical Method and Law" by legal scholar John Dewey. He brings up a commonly cited simpleton syllogism as an illustration of logic-based thinking, which is that since all men are mortal, and Socrates is a man, we can therefore conclude that Socrates is mortal.

This highlights the basic foundations of logical argumentation. You have an initiating principle (all men are mortal), there is an instance or fact at hand (Socrates is a man), and we can reach a suitable conclusion accordingly (Socrates is mortal).

Many people would wholeheartedly believe that this is how lawyers think.

But is it?

Not according to author Dewey (side note, construe the adjective use of "he" as he/she throughout this passage from 1924): "No lawyer ever thought out the case of a client in terms of the syllogism. He begins with a conclusion which he intends to reach, favorable to his client of course, and then analyzes the facts of the situation to find material out of which to construct a favorable statement of facts, to form a minor premise. At the same time, he goes over recorded cases to find rules of law employed in cases which can be presented as similar, rules which will substantiate a certain way of looking at and interpreting the facts. And as his acquaintance with rules of law judged applicable widens, he probably alters perspective and emphasis in selection of the facts which are to form his evidential data. And as he learns more of the facts of the case he may modify his selection of rules of law upon which he bases his case."

Getting an AI system to perform in this web-like manner of progression and regression is a lot harder than you might think. The easier approach by far is to abide by the syllogism approach. In fact, the dominant way of devising AI for legal reasoning is to program the system to essentially collect together all the principles (which are luckily pristine and abundant), be fed facts that are assumed as incontrovertible (how fortunate), and then spit out the logically connected conclusions.

Conclusion

Some might be misguidedly generous and contend that this is *nearly* equivalent to thinking *like* a lawyer, but that lax and loosey-goosey representation is a rather desperate contention. All told, ongoing efforts to derive AI that can think like a lawyer have a long road ahead.

We'll have to wait and see if we can get AI to someday "think" as a lawyer and not simply think kind-of-sort-of like a lawyer.

Note: *For supplemental materials depicting the aspects discussed in this chapter, refer to Appendix B, which contains various augmented diagrams, charts, and additional related facets of relevance.*

CHAPTER 12
AI & LAW:
LEGAL ENGINEERS

Key briefing points about this essay:

- Hiring for legal engineers remains brisk and the outlook is assuredly sunny
- There is some confusion in the marketplace about the role of a legal engineer
- They blend the combined expertise of software engineering and the legal realm
- A non-profit professional association exists, the American Society of Legal Engineers (ASLE)
- Legal engineers will continue in demand, even in light of no-code and low-code efforts

Introduction

Take a look at any of the various job ad boards in the legal profession and you'll likely see an abundant and nearly desperate clamoring call for legal engineers.

Finding a legal engineer is rough to do since they are pretty much as scarce as hen's teeth.

In addition, there is a bit of confusion in the marketplace about what a legal engineer does, along with uncertainty about the appropriate qualifications for someone to tout the vaunted title of being a legal engineer.

Let's back up a moment and first clarify why there is an existent need or calling for the use of legal engineers.

I'll begin with a hopefully inarguable truism, namely that technology has increasingly become a vital part of the legal ecosystem. For most lawyers, jurists, and other participants in the legal world, high-tech has been inching further and further into the practice of law. Not everyone necessarily embraces the incessant march toward more and more tech in the law. That being said, as the sage adage goes, you might as well not tilt at windmills and instead summarily accept that high-tech is here to stay and will continue to expand its reach and impact upon the legal realm.

If you are still with me on this emphatic point, the next somewhat obvious question is who will aid in the necessary tasks of devising, implementing, and maintaining all of this legal high-tech. There isn't any magic pixy dust that will give rise to the tech.

Even for those that wish to buy off-the-shelf LegalTech wares, you ought to realize and be forewarned that a great deal of added work is required to ensure that newly embraced systems are suitably integrated into your practice. Making crucial investments in what could otherwise become *shelfware*, meaning that you subscribed or bought the tech but it is not actively put into use, undercuts your lawyering efforts and needlessly depletes limited funds.

Plus, you would be wise to have at-the-ready expertise for working shoulder-to-shoulder with your attorneys and other legal professionals in the day-to-day use and ongoing adoption of the tech. Few lawyers will right away welcome new tech and the odds are that a lot of handholding is going to be needed. Furthermore, the handholding will be wasted if the attorneys feel that the person doing the abetment is bereft of knowledge about the law and what lawyers actually do.

Okay, I think you are likely convinced or at least turning the corner toward the notion that someone is needed that can straddle the legal world and the tech world.

Consider these four potential options:

- Use a lawyer that relishes tech
- Use a software engineer that relishes the law
- Pair up a lawyer and a software engineer
- Get a legal engineer (a kind of combined melding)

Those are not mutually exclusive options and a given law office or entity might leverage any of those possibilities at the same time.

A legal engineer is a newer type of role and generally consists of a specialist that has closely intertwined the precepts of software engineering and the keystones of the law and the practice of law. To make that a fairer representation, we could say the same thing in the other order, such that this is a specialist that intertwines the keystones of the law and the precepts of software engineering. The goal is to blend both worlds, doing so adroitly and deeply.

Specialties Of Legal Engineers

I'll add further nuance to this role by pointing out that there can be additional specialties within the overarching specialty per se. In essence, not all legal engineers are the same in terms of their focus or particular expertise.

For example, regarding the advent of AI in the legal field, some legal engineers specifically focus on AI-related aspects, including AI techniques and technologies for the law that entail Machine Learning (ML), Natural Language Processing (NLP), Knowledge-Based Systems (KBS), etc. The job title often used by those experts stipulates that they are "AI Legal Engineers" or perhaps "Legal Knowledge Engineers" (there is also the mouthful "Legal Machine Learning Engineer" title, though rarely used so far).

You might find of notable interest that there is a non-profit professional association known as the American Society of Legal Engineers (ASLE) that is aiding in formulating and spearheading the rise of legal engineers. The ASLE's overall mission is to provide a North Star direction and mindful guidance for the maturation of the legal engineer profession. This is assuredly sorely needed and vigorously welcomed.

The founder of ASLE, Eric DeChant, expressed eloquently what the aspiration involved: "Legal Engineers are trained across scientific and legal disciplines to enable more efficient delivery and access to justice. They abide by a strict moral and ethical code of conduct, which lays out a duty not only to the clients they serve, but to their peers, employers, and (perhaps most importantly) society overall" (in his blog posting entitled "What Is A Legal Engineer").

You might be wondering where the nascent pioneers of early-on legal engineers are ending up.

There are plentiful options.

Some are hired into law firms and primarily work in-house. Some are brought into law firms and used in-house and for outreach purposes, serving in a consultative capacity. Legal engineers are settling into the vendors that make and sell the latest in LegalTech. Consulting firms that assist law firms are grabbing up legal engineers. The courts are bringing in legal engineers. Regulators and legislative teams are adding on-board the inclusion of legal engineers. One of the quickest to snap-up legal engineers are startups that are bringing advanced tech to the legal ecosystem.

Conclusion

Believe it or not, already some skeptics contend we won't need legal engineers in the near future because everything will be so-called low-code or no-code and lawyers will be doing all the tech work on their own (that's the proverbial and controversial lawyers-as-coders mantra).

For anyone worrying that legal engineers are going to summarily become extinct, put that non-sensical notion out of your noggin. By and large, the use of legal engineers is the more cost-effective and productive use of labor in contrast to tasking non-tech lawyers with trying to do the nitty-gritty tech work.

You can decidedly take that to the bank, as they say.

.

Note: *For supplemental materials depicting the aspects discussed in this chapter, refer to Appendix B, which contains various augmented diagrams, charts, and additional related facets of relevance.*

CHAPTER 13

AI & LAW:
CIRCULAR LEGAL REASONING

Key briefing points about this article:

- A potential logic-based fallacy consists of using circular reasoning for your arguments
- The usual approach consists of stating a premise as a fact that later is also the conclusion
- Of course, that can be a flawed way of trying to prove your case
- Lawyers often fall into this same trap, though others such as Einstein have done so too
- AI-based legal reasoning systems can aid lawyers in coping with circular reasoning

Introduction

Imagine a courtroom filled with attendees and participants.

A person accused of a crime is on trial.

The defense attorney gets up, walks over to the jury, and makes an outspoken remark. The esteemed lawyer states categorically and without reservation that his client is assuredly not a criminal, and thusly could not possibly have committed the stated crime.

That pronouncement seems stridently convincing, though it also contains a sublime overabundance of what some would call circular legal reasoning. As mentioned in an NYSBA Journal article by Gerald LeBovits on lawyering techniques entailing logical fallacies, the use of circular reasoning in legal arguments can be dicey. In this particular example about the defense attorney proclamation, LeBovits emphasizes: "The fallacy in the argument — even though reputation evidence is admissible — is that the defendant is innocent just because he's not a criminal. The logic is circular."

We have to be cautious about overanalyzing the one line because there could have been a lot of other contextual narratives that might aid in bolstering the logic involved. Nonetheless, this is a handy illustration of *circulus in probando*, meaning to try and circularly prove something. The usual trickery involves starting with a premise (or sneaking one into a smattering of premises) that is the conclusion you are trying to prove.

If you want to prove that A must be true, you begin by laying a foundation that A is in fact true by definition. Whatever else happens in your logical progression from that premise is ultimately going to allow you to inevitably arrive at the desired conclusion that you are seeking to prove.

In short, I declare that A is true, then blither on regarding a bunch of possibly relevant or even irrelevant mumbo jumbo, and I finally reach a grandiose conclusion that A is decidedly true (due to the logic employed).

Most people will typically fall for this insidious chicanery.

Einstein surprisingly used circular reasoning in his famous paper of 1905 that described the now-classic and ubiquitous formula underlying mass-energy equivalence, namely propounding that E = mc squared. Yes, as unbelievable as it might seem, Einstein managed to embed into his premises the essence of the astounding equation itself. A careful walkthrough of his mathematical logic will show you that his earth-shattering end result is merely a consequence of the starting premise.

I realize that might seem disturbing and you are undoubtedly worried that maybe E does not actually equal the claimed assertion about mass and light.

I'm sure you'll be relieved to know that Einstein's use of circular reasoning was quickly detected by many readers, notably so by the eminent physicist Max Planck. Einstein subsequently issued a second paper that showcased his intended logic in a different manner and demonstrably eliminated the circular reasoning. He had originally fallen into the mental trap of *circulus in probando*, which in the mathematics realm is referred to as *petition principii*, something that has happened repeatedly throughout the entire history of mathematics.

Begging The Question In The Law

Some use the phrase "begging the question" when pointing out that circular reasoning is being utilized. You've likely observed the tendency toward using circular legal reasoning in various legal circumstances. A favorite of mine is this example from the New York Civil Practice Law that attempts to define the meaning of the word judgment by merely circularly saying that it consists of judgment: "Judgment. The word 'judgment' means a final or interlocutory judgment" (as covered in a *Minnesota Law Review* article by George Christie entitled "Vagueness and Legal Language").

You can use circular legal reasoning and oftentimes get away with it, especially if you don't make too large a splash about the premise and conclusion being the same. One of the frequent downfalls that will get you caught consists of using so-called *chronic* circular reasoning, whereby you repeat the deficiency over and over: "But all is not lost if the participant, having made one loop in his argument is able to exit the circle which he has made; much the same as a customer, caught in the revolving door of a business establishment, having made one revolution finds the exit and reaches his destination" (per Gary Colwell on "Freedom, Determinism and Circular Reasoning" in the journal of *Argumentation*).

Lawyers are readily susceptible to divining circular legal arguments.

You might not notice that you have done so, akin to presumably Einstein not realizing initially that he had made such a logic-based foul. Of course, if the logic prevails such that the jury or judge is convinced, you are happy as a clam. Things can get problematic though once the opposing side discovers your flaw and attacks it voraciously.

The use of AI in the law is going to help deal with circular legal reasoning.

An AI-based legal reasoning system can potentially detect when a lawyer is making use of circular reasoning. This could alert you to accordingly take proactive action. If it is your own logic that has the circularity, you might want to excise the circular parts. If it is the legal logic of your opponent, you can brandish the discovered circularity like a skewer and undercut their position.

Conclusion

Consider this final thought and prepare yourself for a conundrum.

Suppose that AI-based legal reasoning systems get good enough to concoct complex legal arguments such that no human lawyering is necessary. Wonderful, some might exclaim. On the other hand, it could be that the AI has landed on circular legal reasoning in making its profound arguments.

Will human attorneys are able to spot the circularity, or might we be lax and allow the AI to get away with *circulus in probando*?

I guess we don't have to worry since the AI isn't going to be circular and therefore won't produce circular results. Wait for a second, that doesn't quite make irrefutable sense.

Note: *For supplemental materials depicting the aspects discussed in this chapter, refer to Appendix B, which contains various augmented diagrams, charts, and additional related facets of relevance.*

CHAPTER 14

AI & LAW: GLUING NLP BENCHMARK

Key briefing points about this essay:

- The use of AI natural language systems has been popularized via Alexa and Siri
- On an overarching basis, these are called Natural Language Processing (NLP) systems
- A core subtopic or element within NLP is Natural Language Understanding (NLU)
- NLP and NLU have gradually been emerging in the legal domain, sensibly so
- A new benchmark dataset known as LexGLUE will help level the playing field

Introduction

Take a moment to think about the last time that you interacted with Alexa or Siri. If you've never had a dialogue with those systems, I'm wondering what cave you might be living in. Perhaps though you've interacted with other lesser-known interpretive systems and maybe didn't even realize that you were doing so.

The advent of everyday use of AI-based Natural Language Processing (NLP) systems has become nearly routine. We take for granted that we can have an interactive dialogue with a machine. Advances in the underlying technology have made NLP capabilities more fluent, faster to respond, and easier to use.

That being said, you would be hard-pressed to sing exorbitant praise for contemporary NLP systems.

Any attempt to engage in a truly effortless discussion between you and the AI system is bound to be exasperating and at times infuriating. The AI does not have a semblance of sentience and thus you need to do all the hard work in getting the NLP to grasp what you are saying. At times, you likely have found yourself restricting yourself to simple words or tightly woven phrases, doing so to aid the AI in gauging what you are emoting.

When referring to NLP all-told, please be aware that there are various subtopics within this larger rubric. For example, some like to say that an especially thorny and crucial subtopic consists of Natural Language Understanding (NLU). The notion is that NLP overall has lots of vital moving parts, though amidst those elements the capacity of performing the "understanding" or doing NLU is the most problematic and toughest nut to crack.

Legal Language And Natural Language Understanding

The legal field has been a hotbed for the use of NLP and NLU.

You might have utilized a LegalTech app that has a natural language front-end to it. This is frequently arising when doing online searches that need to pore through vast stores of legal documents. A search in a massive dataset of legal contracts or perhaps while doing e-discovery can be greatly aided by the use of NLP and NLU. Search efforts will be less arduous, consuming less time by a lawyer, and hopefully finding the right targeted documents in the quickest ways.

Today's natural language analysis via AI is somewhat stymied when it comes to legal documents. As any lawyer knows, the use of legal language consists of somewhat obtuse and arcane words and phrases. Furthermore, the meaning of legal language can be far afield of what non-lawyering language consists of.

Some enterprising souls initially tossed conventional NLP and NLU into the realm of the legal field and did so without particularly honing their wares for the legal profession. In that case, the odds of the AI system being helpful to you were diminished. Oddly enough, the AI could be counterproductive and waste your time. As such, there were disillusioned lawyers that decided to forego using the NLP entirely and reverted back to the usual kinds of cryptic commands-based queries.

I don't fault them for that stepping back.

Imagine that you were trying to communicate with a toddler that didn't speak your language. You would need to make wild guesses about how to say things and try to get the toddler to comprehend you. Back and forth you might go, consuming tons of time. I don't want to overextend this analogy since it could inadvertently anthropomorphize the AI aspects, but I think you get my drift.

For those that are relatively proficient in using blunt and straightforward commands, there is little value in using a stilted NLP that is attached to a law-based search engine or LegalTech app. You find yourself getting lots of false hits and having to wade through superfluous stuff. To some degree, the fault, or shall we say weakness in the NLP is that the legal-focused natural language understanding or NLU component is not up to par.

The good news is that there are a lot of AI developers, startups, academic researchers, and vendors all vying to attain a nirvana version of NLU for the legal field.

The not-so-good news, which I dare say is the bad news, consists of not having a ready means of discerning the wheat from the chaff. You see, the news media that concentrates on the legal field is constantly publishing outstretched headlines of some new NLP or NLU that has finally turned the corner and can fully understand what lawyers utter. I'd highly suggest that you take those proclamations with a huge grain of salt.

What we need is a robust and fully standardized way of being able to assess the AI-based legal language NLP and NLU systems. A benchmark, as it were. This would make the grading or assessment of any given product easy-peasy to do.

Voila, a collaboration by a number of legal scholars has led to the unveiling of the Legal General Language Understanding Evaluation (LexGLUE) benchmark.

In a handy introduction and overview entitled "LexGLUE: A Benchmark Dataset for Legal Language Understanding in English," the researchers explain how they have put together numerous datasets that can be used for evaluating a diverse range of legal-oriented NLU tasks. Authors Ilias Chalkidis, Abhik Jana, Dirk Hartung, Michael Bommarito, Ion Androutsopoulos, Daniel Martin Katz, and Nikolaos Aletras are associated with prominent law schools in the U.S., U.K., Denmark, Germany, Greece, and other locales.

Currently, the legal documents are all in English and future extensions will incorporate other languages. The datasets are openly available on the Hugging Face Dataset archive, while the programming code of the models is available at GitHub (these are popular online sites used for storing data and code). There are presently seven major datasets, labeled as SCOTUS, ECtHR – Task A, ECtHR – Task B, EUR-LEX, LEDGAR, UNFAIR-ToS, and CaseHOLD. The SCOTUS dataset contains the Supreme Court Database (SCDB) that has metadata for all Supreme Court cases from 1946 to 2020.

Conclusion

The beauty of LexGLUE is that it provides a level playing field.

Those of us that want to gauge the performance of any particular AI-based legal-focused NLP or NLU can ask how well the system does on this new benchmark. Of course, some vendors are going to have heartburn, partially since their product might not do well, but also more legitimately they might contend that the type of legal documents and data is not the kind they are aiming to analyze and interpret.

In that case, I urge them to work with LexGLUE and add the appropriate datasets to aid in bolstering the fullness of the benchmark.

Help others and meanwhile help yourself, that's a worthwhile mantra.

Note: *For supplemental materials depicting the aspects discussed in this chapter, refer to Appendix B, which contains various augmented diagrams, charts, and additional related facets of relevance.*

CHAPTER 15

AI & LAW: QUANTUM COMPUTATIONAL LAW

Key briefing points about this essay:

- Existing computers generally continue to use the same hardware design as per the 1950s
- A newer approach consists of quantum computing
- We are in the early days of quantum computers and much still needs to be resolved
- Meanwhile, quantum computing is quite handy for computer uses in the law
- The exciting field of quantum computational law is getting increasing traction

Introduction

Quantum supremacy!

That's what the headlines were blaring a couple of years ago. There had been outstretched efforts to use some still-being-figured out quantum computers to solve mathematically intense problems, ones that conventional computers could not presumably calculate in any suitable timeframe. This led to the clamor that quantum computers were here and supreme.

Not everyone agreed that this contention was properly warranted. Much debate ensued.

Meanwhile, bubbling underneath all that sparkle has been the ongoing pursuit of quantum computational law. There haven't been any grandiose pronouncements and the work primarily consists of heads-down heavy-duty research and experimentation. Mark my words, though, one day there will be a shining light that beams brightly upon the emergence of quantum computational law.

But let's take a step back and clarify what this whole quantum hullabaloo consists of.

Today, our conventional computers pretty much employ the same hardware architecture that they have since the beginning of the computer field. Sure, the hardware has gotten faster, smaller, and cheaper in cost, yet nonetheless, the underlying design principles and operational approach are still intact.

Often referred to as classical computing, you can also be in the know by calling the hardware a Turing machine (named after Alan Turing, a pioneer in mathematics and computing), or at times mumble to your friends and everyday strangers that the hardware is von Neumann architecture (named after physicist and mathematician John von Neumann).

Now that you've gotten that groundwork, it is time to introduce Einstein into this equation.

In physics, there is a field of study known as quantum mechanics. At the atomic and subatomic levels of our universe and matter, aspects are going on that seem to be somewhat mysterious and not readily explained by ordinary physics. Those in the field of quantum mechanics offer indubitably fascinating theories to explain the unusual behaviors occurring at the particle and sub-particle levels.

For example, it appears that particles can be somehow connected with each other when at long distances from each other, and yet there's no apparent reason why the disparate particles should be able to interconnect with each other. Generally, this is known as quantum entanglement.

Einstein was in the middle of the heyday of quantum mechanics formulation. He is famously known for having said that this surprising kind of entanglement is "spooky action at a distance" and fretted over how such an odd phenomenon could be fully explained.

Thus, you can quote Einstein that this whole thing is spooky.

Anyway, the thing is, even if you do or don't buy into the competing theories, the phenomenon itself does appear to exist and therefore we might as well exploit it.

For computers, it was thought that you could construct the bits and bytes, the memory components, utilizing the quantum approach, and potentially be able to dramatically speed up the computer memory capability.

Since this is a different approach to conventional computers, it has become known as quantum computing, consisting of a special computer that leverages the quantum aspects and does so using what are called qubits. Qubits are somewhat akin to classical bits but are revved up on steroids so that they are essentially faster, a heck of a lot faster than today's conventional computers.

Right now, it is extremely expensive to build a quantum computer, it is relatively large, it requires immense cooling, and it has only a few qubits, thus, it isn't anywhere near to its full potential as yet. Of course, you can't go around saying that computers are too big and bulky, which some said during the era of vacuum tubes and predicted that computers would always need an entire room of space, yet today we have smartphones in our pockets that are many times more powerful than the early mainframes.

It is reasonable to assume that quantum computers will ultimately get smaller, more robust, less costly, and so on, though it is going to be many years, likely decades before that happens if it can happen at all.

You might be wondering what a quantum computer can do for you that a classical computer cannot do.

There are certain classes of problems that conventional computing struggles to calculate in any "reasonable" length of time. For example, the famous traveling salesperson's problem of wanting to figure out which cities to visit in the most minimalist way gets nearly mathematically and computationally intractable as the number of cities being considered rises highly. It could take say 10,000 years for a conventional computer to render the needed calculations for large-scale settings.

Quantum computing could potentially do the same calculations in months, weeks, days, or even seconds.

Bringing Quantum To Computational Law

We can use quantum computing in the law and tap into the raw calculative power to potentially take on really tough legal problems. Especially alluring is that quantum computing might make AI-based legal reasoning a more viable proposition.

Quantum computational law is the notion of combining quantum computing with the myriad of efforts seeking to utilize advanced computer systems in the legal field. By the way, we don't have to somehow choose between conventional computing and quantum computing. They both will have applicability and you should not somehow assume that the quantum approach will obviate the need or use of conventional computing.

The initial and most prosperous use of quantum computational law will be whenever there are complex legal analyses requiring optimization. As pointedly described in a recent article by Jeffery Atik and Valentin Jeutner: "The law is replete with multi-factor tests, where judges or legislatures create lists of factors that are to be considered (as a matter of process) or weighed (as in 'balancing tests') before reaching a legal conclusion" (as published in the *Law, Innovation and Technology* journal and entitled "Quantum Computing and Computational Law").

Furthermore, the researchers noted that specialized quantum algorithms will be needed: "These legal optimization challenges may, however, be resolved using quantum computers (assuming appropriate quantum algorithms can be identified for them)." I bring up this especially keen nuance to emphasize that it is unlikely that computational law developers will simply port a conventionally coded program over to a quantum computer. New programming languages are being devised to best exploit quantum computing.

The vaunted "quantum supremacy" is a somewhat imaginary demarcation that posits the presumption that quantum computing will showcase itself as the *supreme* method of computing and overtake conventional computing. This is a line in the sand that serves mainly to inspire interest in quantum computers and otherwise has no special significance per se.

Conclusion

That being said, there are certainly avenues within computational law that likely will only reach fruition by embracing the revered quantum computing capabilities. Not wanting to further propagate a false battle, but I suppose one could assert that quantum computational law might reign supreme over conventional computational law.

Ouch, those are fighting words, for sure.

Note: *For supplemental materials depicting the aspects discussed in this chapter, refer to Appendix B, which contains various augmented diagrams, charts, and additional related facets of relevance.*

CHAPTER 16

AI & LAW: COMPUTATIONAL LEGALISM

Key briefing points about this essay:

- The phrase "computational law" is well-established
- A new phrase that entails a subset has been proffered as "computational legalism"
- Qualms about the similar-sounding naming are worth noting
- Meanwhile, the computational legalism precepts are nonetheless worthy too
- Turns out that AI in the law is likely to aid in mitigating some of those precepts

Introduction

Computational legalism is a new phrase that has the potential for being useful in its content but meanwhile confounding in its naming.

Allow me a moment to elaborate.

There is already a commonly accepted and altogether standardized wording of "computational law" that permeates the field of computers and the law. The newly minted phrasing of "computational legalism" seems misleadingly similar. That does present a bit of a problem for this legalism-phrased new kid on the block.

In any case, we shall not toss the baby out with the bathwater (a bit of a tropism). Let's first start by clarifying what computational law consists of. We can then take a look at computational legalism. Finally, we'll consider the value of the computational legalism content and ruminate on the naming-related conundrum.

We shall begin with computational law.

Computational law is already a well-established field of endeavor, ostensibly encompassing the full range of matters entailing the intertwining of computing capabilities and the law. As per the esteemed Computational Law initiative at the Stanford University Law School, a succinct way to conceive of computational law is that this realm "focuses on the formalization of governmental regulations and enterprise policies, development of automated reasoning procedures for compliance checking, legal planning, and regulatory analysis, and developing user-facing computer systems. More broadly, the envisioned outcomes of the Computational Law project have the potential to bring legal understanding and legal tools to everyone in society, not just legal professionals, thus enhancing access to justice and improving the legal system as a whole" (as stated in the Stanford Law School's Center for Legal Informatics credo).

What then is computational legalism and how does it stack up in comparison to computational law?

In an interesting research paper by Laurence Diver, computational legalism is an extreme form of unreflective rule-following and presents daunting if not dire consequences for the legal realm: "The implications of computational legalism are troubling, particularly in societies where we expect that rules regulating behavior have some connection to democratic processes and ex-post judicial oversight. The central claim, then, is that the standards that make legal norms formally legitimate ought *mutatis mutandis* to be applicable to other normative orders that enable and constrain behavior, regardless of the positive content of those rules (although form will, of course, constrain content)" as published in the journal of *Law, Innovation & Technology* in an article entitled "Digisprudence: The Design of Legitimate Code").

That might seem densely packed, so a modicum of unpacking will be handy to undertake.

There is a trend toward employing program code as a means of embodying our laws. You might have heard about law-as-code, a popular mantra that law itself can be presumably represented in program code.

In addition, another commonly used refrain is code-as-law. This suggests that program code can take on the role of being seemingly surrogate or de facto laws. Note that law-as-code and code-as-law are not the same per se.

A bona fide qualm about code-as-law is that cryptic or arcane program code can be a lot less understandable by both lawyers and non-lawyers, thus hiding laws or otherwise making laws less accessible and nearly inscrutable. Prior to code-as-law, we have traditionally utilized text-based narratives to express our laws, something that has served mankind reasonably well since the invention of laws.

The computational legalism concept wraps together the code-as-law into a bundle that highlights the downsides and impending dangers of a gradual shift toward usurping text-based laws with program code as our laws. Per the research paper, computational legalism consists of six key parameters or factors underlying the dark side of code-as-law, namely code's ruleishness, opacity, immediacy, immutability, pervasiveness, and private production.

AI As Mitigator For The Key Factors

Before jumping into the six factors, allow me a moment to suggest that each of the identified factors can be somewhat mitigated or altogether ameliorated via the advent of AI in the law. The proper and sensible use of AI could countermand much of the angst, though this does not mean that AI is a silver bullet.

With that declaration now clearly on the table, we can turn our attention to the six factors of computational legalism.

Using shortened definitions based on the research paper, here's a quick summary:

- **Ruleishness:** Programmed code will work strictly on a predefined rules basis, per fixed conditions that are predetermined in the code, leading to a rote application of law that is potentially inapplicable to varying circumstances.

- **Opacity:** Program code is inherently inscrutable when it comes to regulative operation, likely amplifying a semblance of legal veiling (society following rules without knowing why).

- **Immediacy:** Rapid and perhaps the roguish speed at which the program code imposes the predetermined configurations of normativity that are embodied in the code.

- **Immutability:** Tendency for the program code to become solidified as a lawful artifact, unchanging and unyielding over time.

- **Pervasiveness:** Ubiquity that one piece of program code regulates innumerable users, or that multiple pieces of code regulate a given user throughout their lifetime.

- **Private Production:** Program code that is devised by private enterprises for commercial gain (rather than the conventional openness of how today's laws are formulated and enacted).

As might be self-evident, all of those factors do present grave concerns about how code-as-law might undermine the law and woefully undercut justice. No doubt about that.

Upon considering the vital notion that code-as-law has both costs and benefits, we would be wise to ensure that we understand the costs or downsides that go along with using program code as law. There are of course benefits to be had too.

I dare say that bundling the matter into a rubric labeled as "computational legalism" is somewhat dicey. This particular phrasing is neither obvious as to intent and nor readily immediately differentiable in the eyes of many that are not already familiar with the similar-sounding "computational law" moniker.

Conclusion

Perhaps a better naming can be divined, especially since the core precept is stridently vital and we ought to mindfully be cognizant of the substantive concerns raised. Some useful repackaging might ensure that the bundle gets needed attention and attraction.

A rose is a rose by any other name, so they say, but then again we already know and have preconceived assumptions about the rose naming, thus better to give way and let the rose be called a rose and call a different flower by an entirely distinctly different name.

Note: *For supplemental materials depicting the aspects discussed in this chapter, refer to Appendix B, which contains various augmented diagrams, charts, and additional related facets of relevance.*

CHAPTER 17

AI & LAW: AI YOU NEED TO KNOW

Key briefing points about this essay:

- AI keeps getting a lot of attention and oftentimes is overhyped
- The use of AI is increasingly being applied into the field of law
- You might be curious as to what the field of AI consists of
- A recent report by the European Commission distills down the essence of AI curricula
- Lawyers knowing what the AI curriculum contains will be prepared when it comes to AI uses

Introduction

The excitement about AI continues to reach higher and higher levels of enthusiasm and gushing accolades. AI is being applied to just about every task that people undertake. This includes the tasks being performed by lawyers and legal professionals.

News headlines in legal publications seem to suggest that AI is getting better and better, including encroaching directly onto the turf of lawyering. Of course, rather than perceiving AI as the enemy and usurping the jobs of lawyers, another viewpoint is that AI will aid attorneys and boost their legal efforts.

There is a great deal of debate about what the notion of Artificial Intelligence or AI per se even consists of.

You see, there isn't an agreed-upon all-encompassing definition of AI and various legislative bills and regulations struggle to pinpoint what the rubric known as AI purportedly entails. Akin to the sage witticism of the blind wise travelers that came upon an elephant and each tried to describe what the creature was, you can come across a multitude of definitions for AI and each definition will likely highlight just a particular portion or element thereof (i.e., just the tail, the trunk, the legs, and so on).

I tend to emphasize that AI is an overarching aspirational aim, serving as a goal that is being avidly pursued by systems developers and AI researchers to produce intelligent-like behavior in machines (showcasing artificially derived intelligence). We aren't there yet and indeed we have no reasonable basis to assume that we will someday achieve sentience in AI.

Right now, we are a far cry from that goal.

But just because we haven't reached the end posts doesn't imply that we can't be leveraging whatever we have come up with so far. Please though know that anyone making outsized claims about what AI can achieve currently is probably selling you some hogwash and swampland to boot.

Anyway, for AI and the law, there are two major avenues of intertwining these two vital fields of endeavor.

The most commonly emphasized intertwining involves adding AI into legal apps or LegalTech. For example, this might include using AI-based Natural Language Processing (NLP) for doing e-Discovery or searching amidst a large corpus of contracts or court cases. Less showy is the application of the law to the emergence of AI systems, whereby legal modes of governance are applied to the design, coding, and fielding of AI apps. Overall, the AI and the law convergence then consists of these two constructs: (1) AI as applied to the law, and (2) the law as applied to AI.

AI Curriculum To The Rescue

Let's somewhat set aside momentarily the vagaries about those myriads of definitions of AI.

If you were going to take a full-blown set of courses about AI, particularly doing so at a university master's degree level, what might those classes encompass?

The typical cornucopia of classes in an AI graduate-level program can aid in illustrating what you might need to know when seeking to become an expert in AI technologies and techniques. That being said, I am not suggesting and nor urging that lawyers personally opt to tackle the depth and underlying engineering facets in such a comprehensive AI degree program. Only for those that might wish to be Legal Engineers might the effort be worthwhile (see my prior coverage about Legal Engineers).

I would wager that at least being aware of what an advanced AI curriculum contains will provide you with a handy semblance of what the field of AI itself portends. A recent report by the European Commission entitled "Artificial Intelligence Masters' Programs: An Analysis Of Curricula Building Blocks" does a great job of surveying a wide swath of AI-oriented graduate degrees and distills them into an all-in-one comprehensive strawman.

The insightful report shapes the AI field into a body-of-knowledge that embodies four major knowledge units:

- AI Essentials
- AI General
- AI Core Areas
- AI Applied Areas

For the *AI Essentials* knowledge unit, the coursework requires learning the concepts, theories, methods, and techniques of computer science that underpin the making of intelligent systems. In addition, a crucial added layer requires getting up-to-speed on probability and statistics.

This makes indubitable sense since much of today's AI systems are based on Machine Learning and Deep Learning, which are computational pattern matching algorithms that rely demonstrably on statistical analyses and probabilities assessments.

The next set of courses in sequence would be the *AI General* knowledge unit. This consists of becoming comfortable with the foundational aspects of AI. As per the report, the intention is to know the building blocks underlying this specialized type of application or system, namely: "Systems designed by humans that, given a complex goal, act in the physical or digital dimension by perceiving their environment through data acquisition, interpreting the collected structured or unstructured data, reasoning on the knowledge, or processing the information, derived from this data and deciding the best action(s) to take to achieve the given goal."

Once you've gotten the *AI Essentials* and *AI General* under your belt, you would be ready to become immersed in the *AI Core Areas*. There are seven core areas that the strawman curriculum delineates. I'll just note that not everyone would necessarily agree that these are the "right" seven, meaning that some AI experts might grumble and claim there are fewer or more core areas, though all-told the list of seven is sufficient and reasonably complete (in my opinion).

The seven core areas are:

- Knowledge Representation and Reasoning (KRR)
- Planning, Search, and Optimization (PSO)
- Machine Learning (ML)
- Natural Language Processing (NLP)
- Computational Perception (CP)
- Robotics, Agents, and Integration (RAI)
- Human-Machine Interaction (HMI)

Finally, the AI Applied Areas segment of the AI strawman curriculum consists of being able to focus AI on a personally preferable or desired application area, such as law, medicine, finance, etc.

There are also two essential applied areas that all ought to include, labeled as "AI Services" and "Philosophy and Ethics of AI" (the former being the hardware and infrastructure for running AI systems, and the latter being the ethical and legal ramifications of AI).

If your law office is considering hiring someone versed in AI to join your legal team, you might want to find out which of the AI curriculum sections they are skilled at. I mention this because some proclaimed AI experts are often only versed in a quite narrow subset or subtopic of AI. Do not fall into the mental trap that someone brandishing the AI moniker knows the full range of AI topics.

Conclusion

You likely would not assume that a lawyer was versed in all subspecialties of law, and nor should you make that kind of assumption about alleged AI specialists. Keep in mind too that there isn't any notable licensing or certification for those that wave the AI shingle as their skillset or profession.

Be wary and also informed about the gamut of what today's AI constitutes, allowing you to make prudent decisions when it comes to hiring for AI acumen or when buying legal apps that profess to embody AI functionalities.

You are now in the know about AI.

Note: *For supplemental materials depicting the aspects discussed in this chapter, refer to Appendix B, which contains various augmented diagrams, charts, and additional related facets of relevance.*

CHAPTER 18

AI & LAW: SUSTAINABLE LEGAL INFORMATICS

Key briefing points about this essay:

- Everyone seems to continually refer to the bottom-line
- There is also a trend toward considering the triple-bottom-line or TBL
- Another way to refer to the TBL is to speak of sustainability
- When infusing AI into the law, the TBL or sustainability have not been top-of-mind
- The pell-mell rush toward AI in the law decidedly needs sustainability considerations

Introduction

We are always being asked to focus on the bottom line.

If you are doing legal work for a client, the bottom-line might be whether you've found a means to satisfy their legal needs. For a law practice, the bottom-line might be how the firm is doing financially and whether it can meet its bills.

Are you familiar with the triple-bottom-line (TBL)?

Don't feel bad if you've not heard of this before. You would need to be more of an accountant or finance wizard to probably be routinely familiar with the triple-bottom-line.

There are customarily three key bottom-line elements in the TBL, consisting of Planet, Profit, and People. You are welcome to sequence those three P's into any order that you like (you can boldly proclaim it as Profit/Planet/People, People/Profit/Planet, etc.). The crux is that they are supposed to all be considered equals and none is greater or lesser than the other.

Some prefer to rattle off the 3 Ps rather than using the more accounting-like TBL acronym. That being said, not everyone necessarily even agrees that the triple-bottom-line hallmark is solely and completely described via the 3 P's alone. But let's not debate that acrimonious matter herein. Instead, for sake of carrying on this particular discussion, we can reasonably stipulate that the 3 P's are adequate to our needs.

To further elucidate the Planet, Profit, and People collective, consider these convenient definitions:

- Planet refers to the belief that we need to be environmentally and ecologically aware and make sure that organizations and society take into account the bottom line of being good to the Earth.

- Profit denotes the usefulness in attaining a positive economic bottom-line that will ensure organizations and society are adding value to whatever they undertake.

- People entail a resolute effort of attaining social equity amidst humanity, requiring companies and society to treat all human capital with appropriate respect, fairness, and equality.

When assessing how well a company or other entity is doing as a global citizen, you might ask for their triple-bottom-line. Are they doing the best that they can do for the planet? Are they earning a profit such that they can remain underway as an ongoing presence? Are they consistently and explicitly paying attention to social equity? Thus, rather than perhaps concentrating exclusively on profit (the traditional singular metric of focus), we have an expectation these days that societally responsible entities are to balance and support all three of the Ps.

How is your law firm or law practice doing on the triple-bottom-line metrics?

I'll leave that to you as a follow-up to ponder and explore.

Meanwhile, another wording likewise encompasses the TBL notion including those cornerstone P's, namely the ostensibly ubiquitous reference to *sustainability* is considered approximately the same thing. Once again, this might cause some pundits to have a bit of heartburn. They might contend that sustainability consists of three dimensions, which are the economy, society, and the environment.

I dare say that we can equate Planet with the environment, Profit with the economy, and People with society. In short, sustainability on a micro-level is reasonably applied to specific entities, while on a macro level the wider scope of the environment, the economy, and society are certainly suitable catchwords bundled into planetwide sustainable aspirations.

We can ergo recast the earlier question about your law firm or law practice and ask whether it is abiding by and embracing *sustainability*.

You be the judge.

AI And Sustainability In Legal Informatics

Shifting gears, I'm keenly interested in applying AI to the law and the practice of law (we'll tie in the sustainability topic shortly, hang onto that thought).

You must be at least somewhat aware of how AI is gradually entering into the legal field. For example, you might have recently used an AI-based Natural Language Processing (NLP) system for doing e-Discovery or searching amidst a large corpus of court cases. Perhaps you used an AI chatbot that aided you in composing a legal contract that you were tasked with doing for a client. And so on.

Researchers and academics tend to refer to the use of computing in the law as being a field of study known as Computational Law (CL). An almost interchangeable phrasing consists of referring to this overall line of inquiry as Legal Informatics (LI). Either way, you can think of AI and the law as a specialty within the computational law or legal informatic realm. The AI element is essentially considered a particular form of computing or informatics, and sits amongst a variety of other technological specializations (e.g., blockchain, virtual reality, and others) that can be applied to the law.

I have dragged you through this seeming tangent to bring you back to the fundamental question about sustainability. When AI is applied to the law, we ought to be thinking about the sustainability therein. Return to the triple-bottom-line. If an AI-infused legal app is doing the right things, we should expect it to be adhering to the Planet, Profit, People precepts.

This expectation is gradually gaining traction.

A recent call for papers in a notable journal that is devoted to sustainable computing has laid out this pertinent definition: "We define the term 'sustainable LI' as an effective legal system, which is enriched and equipped with the best computing and informatics techniques and technologies and consequently is faster, fair, tractable, democratic, economically feasible and accessible even to the last person of the underrepresented, underprivileged, and marginalized sections of society" (per the *Sustainable Computing: Informatics And Systems* journal).

You might be thinking that it seems obvious that sustainability should be on the top of mind for those integrating AI into the legal realm.

Sorry to say, it has not especially been a high priority per se.

As insightfully mentioned by the editors for this upcoming special issue focusing on Sustainable Legal Informatics, the application of AI into CL and LI is still just at its infancy: "Although, the usage of general AI in law research is not new, but has largely remained very thin, which can be dubbed as Infant LI; however, its intensity has increased since organizations' massive digitalization, including the legal institutions and administrations."

Conclusion

We have no time to lose and must get sustainability into the mindset and vital measures for those crafting and fielding AI-based legal apps and LegalTech. To some degree, the horse is already poking out of the barn. Before the horses go free and become chaotically and dangerously wild, we must illuminate and propagate the importance of incorporating sustainability.

Better late than never, so let's energetically push forward on sustainability when it comes to AI in the law.

Note: *For supplemental materials depicting the aspects discussed in this chapter, refer to Appendix B, which contains various augmented diagrams, charts, and additional related facets of relevance.*

CHAPTER 19

AI & LAW: SHORTCOMINGS OF THE AI ACT

Key briefing points about this essay:

- Regulators have their eye on AI
- Well-documented examples of AI containing inherent biases and inequities have arisen
- The European Commission has floated a draft regulation, the Artificial Intelligence Act (AIA)
- Europe and other countries around the globe are bound to use the AIA as a cornerstone
- Meanwhile, recent evaluations have shown that the AIA draft has some vital flaws

Introduction

Making and passing legislation can be a tricky affair.

There are often calls for ensuring that the regulations are ostensibly *perfect*, though the strident viewpoint of what might be classified as vaunted perfection will differ tremendously from stakeholder to stakeholder.

That being said, an especially imperfect regulatory imposition can be quite dicey and altogether troubling. There is a significant chance that a newly passed legislative act might be nightmarish overregulation and be oppressive and dampening to society. On the other hand, if a regulation turns out to be sorely underregulating, perhaps whatever was supposed to get curtailed or mitigated continues to run wildly and without proper oversight.

One supposes that the goal would be to achieve a Goldilocks balance, namely that a regulatory codification should be just right. There must not be porridge that is overly cold or overly hot. We presumably don't want overregulating aspects and nor underregulating aspects. The legislature ought to ergo strive toward wording, meaning, and enactment that is at the ideal temperature, as it were.

I bring up this conundrum about passing new legislation due to the recent push toward regulating AI.

You might not know that there is a global urge to put AI in its place. Governments are worried that AI systems are being rolled out with abandon. Indeed, there are plenty of well-documented instances of AI that are riddled with racial biases, gender biases, and altogether completely misses the mark on diversity and equity. We had started with a blissful *AI For Good* mantra, and now we are discovering the dreadful underbelly of *AI For Bad.*

Some proffer the excuse that you have to expect the good to be accompanied by the bad.

In short, if you want all the nifty innovations that AI systems can provide, you must also begrudgingly accept that there are going to be sore spots and bad apples in the proverbial AI barrel. Do not summarily and prematurely quash the advent of AI by trying to enact punishing legislation. All that will happen is that AI will dry up and we'll be devoid of the cherished benefits due to AI-infused apps.

Nonsense, some say in retort to such an argument.

There is a means to guide and grow the building and fielding of AI toward a shining light of goodness. And in the same breath, it is possible to stridently penalize those that provide AI of a societally unappetizing or downright insidious nature. The right kind of regulatory controls will allow us all to have beneficial AI and simultaneously restrict or expunge the unsavory kind of AI.

Poking At The Artificial Intelligence Act

One of the most prominently proposed sets of AI regulations was unveiled by the European Commission earlier this year. The draft is commonly referred to as the Artificial Intelligence Act or abbreviated simply as AIA. Many pundits believe that the formally floated but not yet passed AIA will serve as a role model for the entire European realm, and likely also be a North star for countries across the globe.

As goes the AIA, so goes the rest of the world's AI legislative efforts and intent.

Of course, not everyone agrees that the AIA is the best thing since sliced bread. Sure, there are bound to be some countries that willingly adopt the AIA wording on a word-by-word basis. Other countries will make rather mild and token changes. Some countries will utterly overhaul the AIA wording and seek to make their own style of AI legislation. A few countries might even decide to toss out the AIA and proclaim that it is worthless and has no credence whatsoever.

That's the way the legislative and regulatory ball bounces across our great planet Earth.

A select group of members in the Robotics and AI Law Society (RAILS) opted to take a magnifying glass to the AIA and dissected the draft accordingly. The author's Martin Ebers, Veronica Hoch, Frank Rosenkranz, Hannah Ruschemeier, and Björn Steinrötter have published their assessment in a multidisciplinary journal known by the single letter *J*, doing so in an article entitled "The European Commission's Proposal for an Artificial Intelligence Act—A Critical Assessment by Members of the Robotics and AI Law Society (RAILS)."

On a bottom-line basis, the researchers generally favor the AIA wording, though there are some serious gotchas and shortcomings to be dealt with, as per their review: "We particularly appreciate that the AIA follows a risk-based approach by imposing regulatory burdens only when an AI system is likely to pose high risks to fundamental rights and safety. However, a closer analysis shows that the proposed AIA may need improvement in many areas."

A major takeaway is that this is a ship that might have a few holes or dents but otherwise appears to have what it takes to be reasonably shored-up and then shakily launched into the AI rocky seas. Better still would be to ensure that the raised concerns are fully fixed or ameliorated prior to passage, and likewise that anyone else seeking to leverage or reuse the AIA ought to be steering clear of the now-identified failings or loopholes.

A quick sample of numerous key concerns include:

- The definition of AI systems is overly broad and bodes for problematic disputes and confusion
- An implication exists that AI subcomponents might go scot-free due to a focus on whole-AI systems
- AI researchers could be at risk since there are no allowed exceptions akin to Art. 89 GDPR
- References to where AI is "located" is ambiguous and territorially worrisome
- Various aspects are ill-defined or undefined, such as "subliminal technique" and "materially distorting"
- Lack of attention and inclusion of individual rights as per AI high-risk perils

- It is unclear whether Member States are locked-in or allowed to deviate from the AIA provisions
- The AIA relies substantially on Art. 114 TFEU (other regulations) but this is murky quicksand
- Etc.

Another overarching qualm is that the AIA focuses especially on so-called high-risk AI systems. Though the AIA valiantly tries to stipulate what that consists of, a veritable Mac truck can be legally driven through the cornerstone indication. Thus, devious AI makers that want to circumvent the AIA will indubitably find clever ways to portray their AI as something less than a presumed high-risk AI system.

Conclusion

There are lots more gotchas worthy of attention.

One last one, for now, involves a key provision that human oversight will be a strident element in limiting the advent of bad AI. This is a nebulous loosey-goosey notion and the AIA wording is bereft of specifics about who, when, where, how, and (to some degree) why this is to be undertaken.

For those the cherish the draft AIA, please don't take these analyses as arrows to the heart. We are all in this together and the use of constructive criticism ought to be welcomed with open arms to ensure that AI is regulated in the right Goldilocks manner.

Note: *For supplemental materials depicting the aspects discussed in this chapter, refer to Appendix B, which contains various augmented diagrams, charts, and additional related facets of relevance.*

CHAPTER 20

AI & LAW: AGED OUT AI PREDICTIONS

Key briefing points about this essay:

- Lots of pundits make predictions that they never have to own up to
- In the tech field, there have been some predictions that ended up aging poorly
- Since the first days of applying AI to the law, there have been predictions thereof
- It is worthwhile to take stock of those predictions and see the latest status
- We can also consider how those predictions will far further ahead in time

Introduction

You've likely heard or seen predictions that caught your fancy. People are generally seeking ways to know what the future holds. We all want to know beforehand the nature of future events and notable possibilities.

Many predictions are made that no one later on figures out were off base or entirely incorrect.

In essence, pundits and other soothsayers can frequently get away with wildly wrong predictions, scot-free. They garner a lot of wide-eyed influential attention at the time of rendering the prediction. Years later, they remain silent about their prior mistaken predictions, and luckily for them, they are unlikely to get called on the carpet for their woefully off-target prophecies.

In the tech field, you might know that there are numerous and quite infamous predictions that ultimately did come back to haunt the person that uttered the audaciously outsized future forecast.

Examples include a noted quote from the 1970s by a major computer maker that there is no reason that anyone would want a computer in their home. In 1995, a well-known tech expert predicted that the Internet would soon fade from popularity and we would no longer care or use the darned thing. Meanwhile, in 2006, tech wizards were proclaiming that Apple would never come out with a mobile phone and, even if Apple did so, it would be a complete flop (a year later, the iPhone was released and subsequently rose to stardom).

Another tech-related field that has had its fair share of inaccurate predictions entails the realm of AI and the law. Yes, there have been ongoing and brazen prophecies about how Artificial Intelligence will revolutionize the law domain. These outsized claims go back to the earliest days of applying AI to the legal profession and the practice of law.

Keystone Predictions About AI And Law

Let's go ahead and tackle some of the keystone predictions that have been made about AI and the law.

I provide them in semi-random sequence herein and you can construe them as all equal in their potency or priority. This list doesn't include all of the myriads of such predictions. You can readily unearth more. Hopefully, this provides a representative sampling and also showcases the topmost ones that garner the greatest visibility and stoke the strongest argumentation.

- Robo-judges

This is the repeatedly exhorted notion that AI will replace human judges. As you know, this hasn't happened. Realistically, we can certainly expect that AI will inevitably aid and augment human jurists. There is also the distinct and real possibility that for certain minor classes or categories of legal cases we might resort to using AI as a surrogate judge.

- Robo-lawyers

Akin to the aforementioned robo-judges, the idea here is that human lawyers will be replaced by AI. Again, you should absolutely anticipate that AI will aid and augment human attorneys, no doubt about that. Furthermore, the odds of using AI-based chatbots and other such legal reasoning systems for legal advisement for relatively modest classes or categories of legal matters are in the cards. The wholescale replacement of human barristers via AI is a prolonged long-term possibility, which some will decry and others likely relish.

- Law is just rules mantra

During the early days of trying to apply AI to the act of legal reasoning, bubbling enthusiasm suggested that the law is merely a collection of rules. If you just surface all the rules and somehow codify them or embody them in a computer system, you will voila have AI-based full-fledged legal reasoning (per the use of expert systems or knowledge-based systems). No such luck. The law and the practice of law are much more than a smattering of arcane rules.

- Law-as-code takeover

This is a variant related to the *law is just rules* proviso. In today's parlance, the belief by some is that the law is nothing more than programming code. We presumably can input the law in that manner and find ourselves having active and lively laws that are interactive and responsive. Those in this camp are welcome to keep trying. We have yet to witness that this is the solution.

- AI fluency in legalese

We all know that generic Natural Language Processing (NLP) keeps getting better and better. Your daily interaction with Siri or Alexa is suitably indicative of how far we've come. Whether this AI fluency can sufficiently function in the legal domain is an open-ended question. Sure, NLP for searching legal documents is likely helpful. We have yet though to see AI fluency that nears any semblance of human attorneys and their use of natural language.

- Lawyering unemployment due to AI

Some have said that the rise of AI in the legal field will produce layoffs and widespread unemployment amongst human lawyers. The belief is that an AI-armed attorney can potentially do the work of ten lawyers, via the use of AI. We've not reached that juncture. Even if do have AI that is so empowering, we do not necessarily know that fewer lawyers will be needed. There might be induced demand for lawyering that comes out of the woodwork.

- Clients will prefer AI over human attorneys

One prediction is that clients will savor dealing with AI and eschew interacting with human attorneys. This is half right. There will undoubtedly be *some* clients that will prefer the ease and access of AI-based legal reasoning systems. That being said, it seems unlikely that *all* clients will shift in that direction.

- Access to justice will prevail due to AI

This is the grand prize of aspirations for AI in the legal domain. Whereas today the barriers to getting legal representation are somewhat daunting, including the cost, availability, etc., the hope is that online AI legal reasoning would overcome those hurdles. Access to justice would be unfettered. Of course, we are not anywhere near to that hoped-for result.

Conclusion

I don't want to get caught by my own words and be later on shown as faltering in making predictions. As such, please be aware that I am not saying that the aforementioned predictions will never come true. They are all-time-based and many of the predictors were earnestly excited about a rapidity in advancing AI to attain outstretched uses in the law.

Best to check in with me in about fifty years and see anew where things stand.

Note: *For supplemental materials depicting the aspects discussed in this chapter, refer to Appendix B, which contains various augmented diagrams, charts, and additional related facets of relevance.*

CHAPTER 21
AI & LAW: LAWYER REPUTATION

Key briefing points about this essay:

- We probably can agree that the reputation of a lawyer is vital to their success
- Those that establish outstanding reputations are going to attract clients
- A reputation that stinks is presumably going to repel clients or not attract them
- Some are seeking to use AI to computationally calculate the reputation of human lawyers
- It could be that AI essentially decides whether you get clients or not

Introduction

Are you the type of person that relishes a good old-fashioned Halloween scare?

I hope so.

Here's something that is bound to raise the hair on the back of your neck: *AI is going to ascertain your livelihood as a lawyer and ostensibly determine whether your vaunted law practice succeeds or flops.*

Say what?

Heck, what kind of ghostly powers does AI have that it can command such a momentous semblance of control over lawyering and the existence of being a human lawyer?

Simply stated, AI is increasingly going to be used to assess and report on the alleged reputation of lawyers, everywhere, and do so by whatever whim of an algorithm that somebody might opt to deploy.

Here are the ghastly details.

We'll begin with the importance of your reputational glow and then identify how AI empowers or stomps on that lawyering make-or-break impression.

I'm sure that you would ardently agree that the reputation of a lawyer is indubitably crucial to their potentiality of earning bucks as an attorney. If you have a dour reputation then clients are presumably not going to be banging on your door to acquire your legal services. A lawyer with a stellar reputation is seemingly going to be raking in the dough, assuming that their reputation is promulgated sufficiently that prospective clients know of the reputational honor badge per se.

In short, there are two key factors. First is the tagging of a reputation to an attorney. Second is the broadcasting or communicative dispersion conveying the nature of the reputation so garnered.

There are lots of online websites that promise to establish and bolster your reputation. Some of those reputational crafting sites will aid in constructing your web presence, such as building a suitable web landing page for you or scouring the web to find and attempt to expunge any foul aspersions marring your reputation. The use of social media is a likewise notable means of trying to shape your reputation.

The list of reputational stoking factors is somewhat lengthy.

Consider this sampling of reputational considerations:

- Are there any client testimonials about you?
- Are there any awards or honors that celebrate your prowess as an attorney?
- Have you been reviewed in any Yelp-like manner and do you have a glittering 4-star or 5-star rating?
- How often have you been quoted or at least mentioned in the plethora of legal beagle news?
- Are you known as a shrewd practicing attorney?
- Have you also been noted as a thought leader in the legal realm?
- What perchance do other attorneys and perhaps jurists too have to say about your command of the law?
- And so on.

In theory, a prospective client is going to try and ferret out your reputational standing, doing so before they commit to exploring their legal case with you. Any attorney that has a big fat zero in the reputational game is unlikely to readily have clients eagerly pursuing them. An attorney with a rotten reputation will be career-limited in what they can achieve.

Furthermore, just having a high and mighty reputation isn't the end-all since you need to ensure that the reputation is known to the world at large. A client that cannot divine that you have a wonderous reputation is going to walk past you and find someone that has one in flashing lights. Thus, you need to make sure that your reputation is in existence and that it is findable or being spread wherever prospective clients are doing their looking.

The Specter Of AI In Lawyering Reputations

Into this story walks the fearsome specter of AI.

Rather than prospective clients having to dig deep to figure out your reputation, they will gradually and inevitably be using AI tools that do this for them.

Currently, a potential client can do a by-hand Google-like search to quickly see what the online socio-sphere has to say about you. The problem with this approach is that the myriad of facts, half-facts, and distortions are usually overwhelming. Trying to make sense of it is daunting.

Some enterprising AI developers think that we ought to let AI do the yeoman's work and calculate your reputation via advanced mathematical formulas and arcane computational pattern matching.

The AI would gather together as much data that it can easily obtain about you, and then crunch it into a final reputational score or narrative. This would happen in real-time. Unlike some of the reputational scoring systems being used today that are based on static data and have dated results, this kind of active AI would do the online analysis at the moment that a prospective client entered their request.

On top of that aspect, the AI would ask the inquisitive prospect about their presumed legal case.

Based on an extensive computational analysis of the case particulars, the AI would then cull through the curated set of lawyers that might seem applicable to the circumstance at hand (using various probabilities and statistical elements). The AI demonstrably becomes the frontline determiner of which lawyers will get their name at the top of the list versus being buried somewhere at the bottom. This makes life easy-peasy for the client that wants to crucially know which if any attorneys they ought to employ.

Does this AI grandmaster make you queasy?

Attorneys presumably prefer to spend their time practicing law, rather than having to fret about what their reputational scoring consists of. Nonetheless, you need to face up to the cold hard fact that AI is going to be shaping what kind of legal work lands at your desk.

One supposes that there will be savvy marketers that will offer to try and trick the AI into making sure that you reside at the top of culled analyses. If the underlying AI algorithm can be reversed engineered or somehow deduced, it might be possible to plant enough data seeds to get the AI to give you an especially glowing reputational indication.

That being said, you can bet that not all attorneys will take these matters entirely lying down. The odds of some form of lawsuits or legal action toward the AI proffering services that do these reputational explications are surely in the cards. Legal arguments will be proffered that this is all a bridge too far.

Conclusion

Anyway, please enjoy your upcoming Halloween celebrations.

Just make sure that whatever you do during your Halloween merriments contributes to your reputation and doesn't undercut it, which the AI is ominously likely to uncover so there is little use in trying to desperately hide it from the all-knowing all-telling omnipresent AI.

Note: *For supplemental materials depicting the aspects discussed in this chapter, refer to Appendix B, which contains various augmented diagrams, charts, and additional related facets of relevance.*

CHAPTER 22

AI & LAW: AI JUDGING JUDGES

Key briefing points about this article:

- Trial court cases are routinely appealed and then reviewed by appeals level judges
- You rightfully assume that the appeals level judges are humans
- Some believe that we will inevitably have AI that takes on that role
- The AI would be allowed to affirm or remand the case
- Further levels of appeal would consist of human judges (for now)

Introduction

Your case didn't go the way that you had hoped. There seem to be sufficient grounds to launch an appeal. The hope is that an appeals judge will see that the case has a serious defect or legally compelling issue that will turn around the ruling closer in your direction.

Judges at the lower courts are abundantly aware that at some point their judgment is bound to be called into question on appeal.

This means that other judges will weigh in on the judging and the eminent judgment made by the lower court judge. Of course, the judges that do that judging are equally likely to ultimately be judged by other judges at even higher levels of the court.

All told, the judging of judges carries up to the pinnacle of the U.S. Supreme Court. One might say that the buck stops there, though indubitably even their judgment will certainly get potentially judged by future Supreme Court judges (perhaps years or decades later).

Lawyers are well aware of the cascading ladder of judging by judges.

To some degree, an attorney that has lost a case will at times be betting that those judges above other judges will see the light and turn the fat zero into a brazen win. If at first, you don't succeed, try and try again, that's the mantra of rendering an appeal.

I assume that whenever I've herein been referring to judges, you naturally and instantaneously were thinking about humanoids. Ergo, human judges oversee other human judges.

Seems blatantly obvious.

Suppose that I was to tell you that we might end up with AI that judges some of those human judges.

Say what?

Yes, there are some legal scholars and legal landscape soothsayers that believe we will gradually opt to use AI as a means of judging judges. Envision that a trial court judge has completed a case (wherein the judge was a human judge). The defendant is on the losing end of things. The attorney for the defendant files an appeal, which goes directly to an AI legal reasoning system that is serving in the capacity of a machine-based judge.

AI That Judges Those That Judge

The AI reviews the case.

In much the same way that human judges would assess the intricacies of the adjudication aspects, so would the AI system. The result could be that the AI finds nothing afoul or akilter and thus reaffirms the ruling of the trial court judge. On the other hand, the AI might detect something legally of substantive concern and proffer that the case must be remanded back to the trial court. This would ostensibly include instructions about how to remedy the issues or errors that were identified.

Whether the AI would be empowered to completely overrule a judgment and summarily dismiss the case is perhaps a bridge too far for some. Having an AI that is judging judges can only go so far, critics assert, and we have to be mindful of inadvertently allowing an overreach of an AI system.

Today's judges are likely to blast this notion of using AI to judge a human judge.

How dare a machine per se be considered "better" than a human, especially in the complex matters entailing human justice. The odds are that contemporary judges would label the whole proposal as pure balderdash or hogwash.

For clarification, we indeed do not have any AI as yet that could appropriately serve in such a capacity. Through extensive research efforts are aiming to produce legal reasoning-based AI systems, those attempts are a far cry from being able to sufficiently perform in the role of a judge, let alone sitting above human judges as a judge of their judgments.

Some would insist that we need to first showcase that AI can in fact sit as a trial judge.

Once we've gotten that far along, we can then begin to speak of using AI-based judging systems to review the cases of human judges. See my prior columns that depict how AI is being crafted to serve at the lower courts in modest ways as a judge or as a supplemental tool for human judges.

There is also the slippery slope conundrum that bothers many about the application of AI for judging judges. How far up the chain will the AI judging occur? If we let an initial appeal go to an AI system, the next thing you know we'll be up to our eyeballs in AI throughout the entire appeals process.

Heck, these critics exhort, you might as well contend that the U.S. Supreme Court will be replaced by AI.

The moment that you let AI peek into the door of the courthouse, you are on a lock-and-step march toward AI being at the topmost summit of the land. It is akin to the famous sage story of the camel that poked its nose into a tent. The next thing the tent occupants knew, that camel has muscled its ways fully into the tent and there is no room left for the human tenants.

Nonsense, the retort goes, you cannot try to douse the use of AI at the initial review level by making outsized claims that the sky is falling and that the legal world will come to an end. That is merely one of those false argumentation tactics. When stoked with fear, the reaction is to stop new innovation in its tracks, they lament.

Would an AI system that reviews the acts of judges be considered a robo-judge?

This is a worthwhile question to ask because there is a lot of adverse baggage already surrounding the *robo-judge* moniker. To escape that grimy quagmire, those advocating AI as a judge of judges would suggest that this is not at all a robo-judge. A robo-judge is purely AI at the trial court level, or so they would like to insist.

Conclusion

Finally, some would argue you need to rethink the AI aspects and not presume that the AI would be working on its own (i.e., fully autonomously).

We could readily use AI as the first stage of an appeal. A human appeals judge would then review the AI "decision" and decide whether to let it stand or override it. This could speed up our legal process and promote greater access to justice. For further analysis of this type of framework, see the engaging article "When Humans Judge Other Humans Using Machines" by Renita Murimi as published in the *MIT Computational Law* journal.

You see, humans and human judges are kept suitably intact and ensure that the AI doesn't go awry. Ponder whether that seems soothing to you, or whether you nonetheless still have serious trepidations about AI that judges the acts of human judges.

Note: *For supplemental materials depicting the aspects discussed in this chapter, refer to Appendix B, which contains various augmented diagrams, charts, and additional related facets of relevance.*

CHAPTER 23

AI & LAW: ONLINE AI COURSES

Key briefing points about this essay:

- Lawyers, jurists, and other legal professionals need to be familiar with AI and the law
- The AI juggernaut is already amidst the practice of law and will continue to accelerate
- Besides reading about AI and the law, consider attending online sessions
- Berkeley Law AI Institute is a notable multi-day morning series coming up in November
- This is a highly interactive set of lectures and panels bringing you up-to-speed

Introduction

I am widely known for my advocacy that lawyers, jurists, and other stakeholders in the legal realm need to become familiar with AI and the law. My numerous columns, books, and seminars on AI and the law abundantly attest to this.

Note that I am not suggesting that AI is necessarily or somehow axiomatically good for the law and the practice of law. It won't be.

There will be lots of bumps and problems along the path of adopting AI throughout the legal realm. For that, I am sure of.

The impacts of meshing together AI and the law will gradually and inexorably shape the future of the vast legal ecosystem and alter demonstrably the day-to-day pursuit of justice. Some refer to AI as a disrupter to the practice of law, while others assert it is transformative and more so complimentary than being perhaps inherently destructive.

Whether you like AI or hate AI, and whether you think AI will be a boon or a bust, the point is that we all need to ensure a lively debate takes place while the AI bandwagon continues to stridently push ahead and dovetail into the law and the daily practice of the law.

There are two primary ways that AI and the law are being intermixed: (1) AI as applied to the law, (2) The law as applied to AI.

The most commonly known aspect entails the use of AI as applied to the law. You've likely used an AI-based computer system when searching a large-scale corpus of legal cases or while doing an especially complex e-Discovery. Akin to the likes of Alexa or Siri, there are Natural Language Processing (NLP) tools tuned to legalese that allow online searches in mammoth legal databases. When developing contracts, you can use AI-infused contract life-cycle management (CLM) to quicken the crafting of a new contract. And so on.

Turning to the other side of the AI and law coin, there is the use of the law as applied to AI. This is generally less exalted than AI-applied-to-law, but nonetheless an important and assuredly serious matter. Do existing laws adequately cover the advent of AI systems of all kinds, including both the *AI For Good* and the *AI For Bad*? As new laws are crafted to cope with the emergence of AI, will those laws be on-target or might they inadvertently overreach? Regulators all told seem bent on trying to rein in the already exposed biases and inequalities embedded into some AI systems, and you can bet that the governance and legal wrangling will expand and become more pronounced over time.

Berkeley Law AI Institute Offering

Besides reading about the burgeoning field of AI and the law, there are various seminars and events that cover the topic too. Be cautious in selecting which learning opportunities you might choose. I say that because there are a plethora of vendor-specific webinars that though are certainly worthwhile when seeking to discover what a particular AI-infused legal system does, you are not likely to get an independently-minded sweeping perspective about the AI and law landscape.

That's something you need to have as a proper grounding for then further exploring the myriad of offshoots regarding AI and the law.

I would also suggest that since you are indubitably obligated to get your MCLE credits under your belt, probably best to do double-duty by learning about AI and the law while also earning those vaunted credits. A match made in heaven, as it were.

One such offering that is coming up next month is annually conducted by my colleagues at the University of California Berkeley via their esteemed Berkeley Center for Law & Technology and the Berkeley Law Executive Education team. Known as the Berkeley Law AI Institute, this is an outstanding set of online interactive sessions that will take place on the mornings of November 2, 3, 4, 9, and 10. Completion of the program will garner up to 18.75 MCLE credit hours by the California State Bar and also earn you a certificate of completion.

Those of you that are aware that I am a Stanford University Fellow might be surprised that I would proffer a recommendation about something or indeed anything at the presumed rival of UC Berkeley (also referred to as Cal). There is a longstanding rivalry as cross-town universities. That being said, I consider my Cal colleagues in the highest light and gladly attest to their outstanding efforts.

Just to clarify, I will though in fact be firmly seated on the Stanford Cardinal side of the Stanford stadium for the upcoming November 20, 2021, so-called "The Big Game" football match between Cal and Stanford (rooting until I am fully hoarse, no doubt). Rest assured on that point.

Returning to the matter at hand, one significant consideration about attending any AI and law courses is whether there is any needed prerequisite, such as needing to beforehand know the tech underpinnings about AI. This can be problematic for some. Lawyers can get caught off-guard by suddenly finding themselves amidst a slew of LegalTech AI-conversant participants and ergo not have any clue about what is being said.

In the case of the Berkeley Law AI Institute, no worries, since the course doesn't have a prerequisite requiring AI-savviness beforehand. Indeed, the first session brings attendees up to speed about AI. Subsequent sessions or modules in the multi-day series are about AI applications in the law, along with implementation facets for putting in place AI systems for law firms and in-house legal teams. The concluding modules discuss societal, ethical, and other legal issues underlying AI uses.

Conclusion

We stridently need more members of the legal profession to get ingrained in the pros and cons of AI and the law. If you decide to merely sit on the sideline and not become engaged, the odds are that you'll be shocked and dismayed when summarily bowled over by some AI legal aiming concoction.

Remember too, the ABA rules of professional responsibility mandate that attorneys are expected to keep up with the latest in *relevant* technology. I'd say there is no argument that AI is exactly that kind of relevancy within high-tech and the law.

Note: *For supplemental materials depicting the aspects discussed in this chapter, refer to Appendix B, which contains various augmented diagrams, charts, and additional related facets of relevance.*

CHAPTER 24

AI & LAW: OVERFITTING MACHINE LEARNING

Key briefing points about this essay:

- The area of *machine learning* is the darling of the AI realm
- Via machine learning capabilities, we've seen a huge expansion in AI-based apps
- This expansion includes AI-infused LegalTech applications
- Note that machine learning is a type of computational pattern matching
- Quite worrisome is that this means that overfitting can occur (buyer beware)

Introduction

Everybody knows that AI has seemingly become the hottest new thing since the invention of sliced bread. Perhaps even more so.

A big part of the emergence of today's AI systems is based on advances made in the subfield known as machine learning. The rubric known as machine learning refers to the various techniques and technologies that are subsumed within the field of AI and that purportedly aid computers in learning how to solve problems of one kind or another.

Please be aware that critics bristle at the moniker of "machine learning" since the use of the word *learning* within that catchphrase can be easily overblown and entirely misleading.

Allow me a moment to explain why this criticism is dutifully bona fide.

When a human learns something, we cannot really say for sure how this takes place. Within our noggin, the brain somehow is able to recalibrate itself and we refer to this as the learning process and ostensibly that the person has learned something. You can debate all day long about how this has occurred within the confines of so-called wetware (that's the colloquialism used to refer to the brain).

All that we can really say is that the outward acts of a person would seem to showcase whether or not they learned the thing that we believe they learned. While in law school, you undoubtedly took lots of tests and quizzes that were designed to try and detect the magnitude of your learning about the law. There wasn't a probe inside your brain that detected this. Instead, only external measures could seek to assess your budding legal prowess.

In short, we cannot fully indicate how the brain learns things.

Shifting gears, the AI field has been trying desperately since its inception to try and craft computer-based systems that can seemingly learn (whatever the act of learning presumably means or implies). If we knew exactly how the brain did this, we could straightforwardly model the mind and then simulate or potentially replicate the same in a machine or computer.

I assure you, describe conclusively how that can be done and you'll easily earn yourself a vaunted Nobel Prize.

In some key ways, our lack of having cracked open or unpacked the inner secrets of how the brain functions are stymieing the advancement of AI. Nonetheless, there are lots of valuable uses for contemporary yet limited AI, including the beneficial application of AI within the field of law and the practice of law.

Machine Learning And Dangers Of Overfitting

What are we to do while we are still searching vigorously to reveal the mysteries of the mind?

The next best thing for right now consists of devising computational pattern matching algorithms that somewhat appear to nudge into the category of being able to learn things. You have to though be extremely careful to suggest an equivalence between those computational pattern matching capacities and the honest-to-goodness kind of learning that humans do.

When I refer to *computational pattern matching*, you might be unsure of what that mouthful of techno-jargon means. An easy way to grasp the nature of machine learning involves harking back to the days that you likely took a statistics course. I would almost bet that you must have been introduced to the use of multiple regression, a rather commonly utilized statistical approach.

You can rightfully think of regression as a type of computational pattern matching. The idea is to feed data into a regression model, out of which you are trying to discern a statistically valid pattern that associates some variable with some other variable. We might for example discover a statistical relationship between a person's height and their weight.

An inherent danger with any computational pattern matching is that it can overfit onto the data presented to the model during the training stage.

One of my favorite explanations for why overfitting is adverse and insidious comes from an example about how an impressionable newbie law student might fall into such a mental trap: "It is as if an entering student meets the members of the law review and learns that they have all been wearing a particular brand of shoes and all sat in the second to last row of Torts and the third row in their Contracts classes. The student thinks they have a perfect theory of what predicts success in school, but obviously, this suffers enormously from retrofitting, which is another way of thinking about overfitting the available data" (as indicated in a fascinating article entitled "The Impact of Artificial Intelligence On Rules, Standards, and Judicial Discretion" by Frank Fagan and Saul Levmore, published in the *Southern California Law Review*).

I'm sure that you've seen many instances of overfitting.

For example, the legal realm reveres the use of precedent, but this can fall victim to the allure of overfitting. Per the research paper by Fagan and Levmore, they emphasize this same qualm that can readily befall our judges and our courts: "If a lower court interprets precedent too loosely and attempts to shoehorn the facts to the rule, then it has overfitted the case; in principle, the error is corrected on appeal."

Those are a plethora or tsunami of illustrative examples of how humans overfit the data that they encounter.

Computational pattern matching algorithms also are vulnerable to overfitting, and perhaps worse so since there isn't any underlying true learning taking place (i.e., lacking human common sense and bereft of human cognition). Machine learning is then an inherently risky proposition to some degree because this now-popular AI approach can overfit without any knowingness occurring, which could produce slyly false results.

Conclusion

Humans need to remain in the loop and oversee the crafting and release of machine learning-based AI.

The use of appropriate by-hand analyses and data and algorithmic probing can aid in surfacing when machine learning has gone overboard, altogether overfitting to the detriment of those humans that are subjected to the AI system being deployed.

Note: *For supplemental materials depicting the aspects discussed in this chapter, refer to Appendix B, which contains various augmented diagrams, charts, and additional related facets of relevance.*

CHAPTER 25

AI & LAW: WET AND DRY CODE

Key briefing points about this essay:

- Law as code is today's popular mantra
- Turns out that the law is not quite the same as programming code
- Some like to refer to wet code and dry code in this context
- A natural language contract would be construed as wet code
- While a smart contract is maybe dry code, or wet code, or something in-between

Introduction

Everywhere you look, lawyers and pundits are talking about law as code, the vaunted aspiration and belief being that the law is altogether the equivalent of programming code.

For example, consider what computer programmers do.

Programmers often write their code using if-then types of statements that certainly seem to resemble rules that you might see in our laws.

Envision a snippet of an existent law that says that if a person does something X, they might have committed a crime Y. By gosh, even a novice programmer could write a program that mimics or mirrors that stated law. In theory, all you need to do is walk through all the laws and ferret out their indicated rules, and then start coding them in a popular programming language such as Python, Java, or whatever.

There is a great temptation to assume that law therefore ought to be easy-peasy for getting coded up into a computer system.

But if you look around, you won't find that to be the case. We do not particularly have our laws altogether coded into computers. Sure, the text of laws is amply available in computer systems, for which you can do a myriad of text-based searches. The searching activity is based on the law as text, rather than the law as code.

One aspect about having law as code would be that you could do more useful things with the law when it is usable online in a code-like fashion. You could ask the computer to crank through the legal logic and see if there are any legal gaps therein. Discovering any such gaps would therefore tend to suggest that the laws themselves have some form of lawfully divined gaps or omissions. Astute lawyers could then use those uncovered gaps to the advantage of their clients and their cases.

Meanwhile, legislators and regulators would presumably become more quickly aware of such gaps in the laws. We can assume that those legal holes would potentially get plugged up rather speedily. Whereas today there is often a lengthy delay before such plugging occurs, the use of computers might radically and dramatically speed up this process. In addition, the courts would seemingly not need to wrestle with the gaps, and nor other ambiguities in the law, since the lawmakers would ably know about legally deficient areas of the law and move to expeditiously deal with the gotchas and guffaws.

The conversion or translation though of natural language-based laws, such as those composed in everyday English (albeit using legalese jargon), presents a greater problem than you might at first glance imagine. Sorry to say that taking our laws and converting them into code is abundantly challenging. This challenge is hard for both humans to do by hand and likewise hard for computers to do programmatically.

AI is hoped to be the potential hero for generating those law-to-code conversions. Perhaps we can use various AI techniques and technologies to translate natural language laws into programming code or something equivalent. We don't necessarily need to have code of the flavor that programmers normally use. It would be fine to target a specialized type of code, perhaps one that is more so structured around the strict principles of logic and logical reasoning (there are numerous such logic-focused programming languages).

Introducing You To Wet Code And Dry Code

You might be somewhat surprised to know that there are some in this field of endeavor that relishes referring to these aspects as *wet code* versus *dry code.*

The catchphrase of wet code is intended to describe our laws in their natural language state. In contrast, dry code is the coding that would be in a computer system as programming code. In short, as per the discussion therein, the goal is to convert or translate wet code into dry code.

I'm betting that you are innately curious about and stridently wondering why the monikers of "wet" or "dry" are being used in this context.

Part of the basis underlies yet another piece of vocabulary often being used, namely wetware. Wetware is a catchy way to mention the human brain and parlays off the conventional hardware and software wordings. Our brains are soaking inside our noggins and ergo the clever or smarmy way to think of things is to say that we think based on our wetware.

If you don't like the brain being characterized as wetware, you aren't alone in your disdain or dismissal of the phrasing. Many don't like it. Nonetheless, since it does have an alluring catchiness to it, the odds are that the terminology will hang around and there is little chance of expunging it.

Let's go ahead and play around with our handy-dandy *wet code* and *dry code* denotations. The result might be useful or at least entertaining.

When you come upon a legal contract that someone wants to have you analyze, the contract would customarily be written in plain old natural language, thus this would be considered as wet code. You would use your wetware (your brain or mind) to assess the contract. Your wetware is examining the wet code.

So far, so good.

You might be aware that there is a burgeoning area of contracts known as smart contracts. These typically are contracts that have been transformed into being online and constructed via the use of blockchain or akin technologies. They are relatively close to the vaunted goal of law-is-code. As such, you could almost declare that smart contracts are dry code.

Then again, if the smart contract has any "smarts" to it, there are some that would argue the smart contract should be labeled as mildly wet code or maybe better still as soggy dry code. The point is that we are presumably starting to blur the lines between pure wet code and pure dry code.

Conclusion

That is quite encouraging.

I render such an assertion because the hope of attaining law as code will be aided and emboldened as we find ways to shift from wet code to dry code, or otherwise intermix the wet code and the dry code portions.

There is though still a long distance to go. We have much to do before expressing tears of joy that we can axiomatically turn wet code into dry code. Someday, there won't be a dry eye in the place once we've achieved such a venerated goal.

.

Note: *For supplemental materials depicting the aspects discussed in this chapter, refer to Appendix B, which contains various augmented diagrams, charts, and additional related facets of relevance.*

APPENDIX A
TEACHING WITH THIS MATERIAL AND BIBLIOGRAPHY

The essays in this book can readily be used as a reading supplemental to augment traditional textbook-oriented content, particularly used in a class on AI or a class about the law.

Courses where this material is most likely applicable encompass classes at a college or university level.

Here are some typical settings that might apply:

- Computer Science. Classes studying AI, or possibly a CS social impacts class, etc.

- Law. Law classes exploring technology and its adoption for legal uses.

- Sociology. Sociology classes on the adoption and advancement of technology.

Specialized classes at the undergraduate and graduate level can also make use of this material.

For each chapter, consider whether you think the chapter provides material relevant to your course topic.

There are plenty of opportunities to get the students thinking about the topics and encourage them to decide whether they agree or disagree with the points offered and positions taken.

I would also encourage you to have the students do additional research beyond the chapter material presented (I provide next some suggested assignments that they can do).

RESEARCH ASSIGNMENTS ON THESE TOPICS

Your students can find research and background material on these topics, doing so in various tech journals, law journals, and other related publications.

Here are some suggestions for homework or projects that you could assign to students:

a) Assignment for foundational AI research topics: Research and prepare a paper and a presentation on a specific aspect of AI, such as Machine Learning, ANN, etc. The paper should cite at least 3 reputable sources. Compare and contrast to what has been stated in the chosen chapter.

b) Assignment for Law topics: Research and prepare a paper covering Law aspects via at least 3 reputable sources and analyze the characterizations. Compare and contrast to what has been stated in the chosen chapter.

c) Assignment for a Business topic: Research and prepare a paper and a presentation on businesses and advanced technology regarding AI and Law. What is trending, and why? Make sure to cite at least 3 reputable sources. Compare and contrast to the depictions herein.

d) Assignment to do a Startup: Have the students prepare a paper or business plan about how they might start up a business in this realm. They could also be asked to present their business plan and should also have a prepared presentation deck to coincide with it.

You can certainly adjust the aforementioned assignments to fit your particular needs and class structure.

You'll notice that I usually suggest that (at least) 3 reputable cited sources be utilized for the paper writing-based assignments.

I usually steer students toward "reputable" publications, since otherwise, they will cite some less reliable sources that have little or no credentials, other than that they happened to appear online was easy to retrieve. You can, of course, define "reputable" in whatever way you prefer, for example, some faculty think Wikipedia is not reputable while others believe it is reputable and allow students to cite it.

The reason that I usually ask for at least 3 citations is that if the student only relies upon one or two citations, they usually settle on whatever they happened to find the fastest. By requiring 3 (or more) citations, it usually seems to inspire them to explore more extensively and likely end-up finding five or more sources, and then whittling it down to 3 if so needed.

I have not specified the length of their papers and leave that to you to tell the students what you prefer.

For each of those assignments, you could end up with a short one to two-pager or you could do a dissertation length in-depth paper. Base the length on whatever best fits for your class, and likewise the credit amount of the assignment within the context of the other grading metrics you'll be using for the class.

I usually try to get students to present their work, in addition to doing the writing. This is a helpful practice for what they will do in the business world. Most of the time, they will be required to prepare an analysis and present it. If you don't have the class time or inclination to have the students present their papers, then you can presumably omit the aspect of them putting together presentations.

GUIDE TO USING THE CHAPTERS

For each of the chapters, I provide the next some various ways to use the chapter contents.

You can assign the below tasks as individual homework assignments, or the tasks can be used for team projects. You can easily layout a series of assignments, such as indicating that the students are to do item "a" below for say Chapter 1, then "b" for the next chapter of the book, and so on.

a) What is the main point of the chapter and describe in your own words the significance of the topic.

b) Identify at least two aspects in the chapter that you agree with and support your concurrence by providing at least one other outside researched item as support; make sure to explain your basis for agreeing with the aspects.

c) Identify at least two aspects in the chapter that you disagree with and support your disagreement by providing at least one other outside researched item as support; make sure to explain your basis for disagreeing with the aspects.

d) Find an aspect that was not covered extensively in the chapter, doing so by conducting outside research, and then offer an expanded indication about how that aspect ties into the chapter, along with the added significance it brings to the topic.

e) Interview a specialist in the industry about the topic of the chapter, collect from them their thoughts and opinions, and readdress the chapter by citing your source and how they compared and contrasted to the material,

f) Interview a relevant professor or researcher in a college or university setting about the topic of the chapter, collect from them their thoughts and opinions, and readdress the chapter by citing your source and how they compared and contrasted to the material,

g) Try to update a chapter by finding out the latest on the topic and ascertain whether the issue or topic has now been solved or whether it is still being addressed, explain what you come up with.

The above are all ways in which you can get the students of your class involved in considering the material of a given chapter. You could mix things up by having one of those above assignments per each week, covering the chapters over the course of the semester or quarter.

SUGGESTED REFERENCES TO EXPLORE

To help get your students started in finding relevant and important papers on the topic of AI and the law, I provide next a handy bibliography that can be utilized.

You could also assign the students to each (or in teams) read an assigned reference from the list, and then have them provide either a written summary and review or do so as part of a classroom presentation.

BIBLIOGRAPHIC REFERENCES

1. Aleven, Vincent (1997). "Teaching Case-Based Argumentation Through a Model and Examples," Ph.D. Dissertation, University of Pittsburgh.

2. Aleven, Vincent (2003). "Using Background Knowledge in Case-Based Legal Reasoning: A Computational Model and an Intelligent Learning Environment," Artificial Intelligence.

3. Amgoud, Leila (2012). "Five Weaknesses of ASPIC+," Volume 299, Communications in Computer and Information Science (CCIS).

4. Antonious, Grigoris, and George Baryannis, Sotiris Batsakis, Guido Governatori, Livio Robaldo, Givoanni Siragusa, Ilias Tachmazidis (2018). "Legal Reasoning and Big Data: Opportunities and Challenges," August 2018, MIREL Workshop on Mining and Reasoning Legal Texts.

5. Ashley, Kevin (1991). "Reasoning with Cases and Hypotheticals in HYPO," Volume 34, International Journal of Man-Machine Studies.

6. Ashley, Kevin, and Karl Branting, Howard Margolis, and Cass Sunstein (2001). "Legal Reasoning and Artificial Intelligence: How Computers 'Think' Like Lawyers," Symposium: Legal Reasoning and Artificial Intelligence, University of Chicago Law School Roundtable.

7. Baker, Jamie (2018). "A Legal Research Odyssey: Artificial Intelligence as Disrupter," Law Library Journal.

8. Batsakis, Sotiris, and George Baryannis, Guido Governatori, Illias Tachmazidis, Grigoris Antoniou (2018). "Legal Representation and Reasoning in Practice: A Critical Comparison," Volume 313, Legal Knowledge and Information Systems.

9. Bench-Capon, Trevor (2004). "AGATHA: Automation of the Construction of Theories in Case Law Domains," January 2004, Legal Knowledge and Information Systems Jurix 2004, Amsterdam.

10. Bench-Capon, Trevor (2012). "Representing Popov v Hayashi with Dimensions and Factors," March 2012, Artificial Intelligence and Law.

11. Bench-Capon, Trevor, and Givoanni Sartor (2003). "A Model of Legal Reasoning with Cases Incorporating Theories and Values," November 2013, Artificial Intelligence.

12. Breuker, Joost (1996). "A Functional Ontology of Law," October 1996, ResearchGate.

13. Bruninghaus, Stefanie, and Kevin Ashley (2003). "Combining Case-Based and Model-Based Reasoning for Predicting the Outcome of Legal Cases," June 2003, ICCBR'03: Proceedings of the 5th International Conference on Case-based reasoning: Research and Development.

14. Buchanan, Bruce, and Thomas Headrick (1970). "Some Speculation about Artificial Intelligence and Legal Reasoning," Volume 23, Stanford Law Review.

15. Chagal-Feferkorn, Karni (2019). "Am I An Algorithm or a Product: When Products Liability Should Apply to Algorithmic Decision-Makers," Stanford Law & Policy Review.

16. Douglas, William (1948). "The Dissent: A Safeguard of Democracy," Volume 32, Journal of the American Judicature Society.

17. Dung, P, and R. Kowalski, F. Toni (2006). "Dialectic Proof Procedures for Assumption-Based Admissible Argumentation," Artificial Intelligence.

18. Eliot, Lance (2020). AI And Legal Reasoning Essentials. LBE Press Publishing.

19. Eliot, Lance (2020). Artificial Intelligence and LegalTech Essentials. LBE Press Publishing.

20. Eliot, Lance (2020). "FutureLaw 2020 Showcases How Tech is Transforming The Law, Including the Impacts of AI," April 16, 2020, Forbes.

21. Erdem, Esra, and Michael Gelfond, Nicola Leone (2016). "Applications of Answer Set Programming," AI Magazine.

22. Gardner, Anne (1987). Artificial Intelligence and Legal Reasoning. MIT Press.

23. Genesereth, Michael (2009). "Computational Law: The Cop in the Backseat," Stanford Center for Legal Informatics, Stanford University.

24. Ghosh, Mirna (2019). "Automation of Legal Reasoning and Decision Based on Ontologies," Normandie Universite.

25. Grabmair, Matthias (2017). "Predicting Trade Secret Case Outcomes using Argument Schemes and Learned Quantitative Value Effect Tradeoffs," IJCAI June 12, 2017, London, United Kingdom.

26. Hage, Jaap (1996). "A Theory of Legal Reasoning and a Logic to Match," Volume 4, Artificial Intelligence and Law.

27. Hage, Jaap (2000). "Dialectical Models in Artificial Intelligence and Law," Artificial Intelligence and Law.

28. Hage, Japp, and Ronald Leenes, Arno Lodder (1993). "Hard Cases: A Procedural Approach," Artificial Intelligence and Law.

29. Hobbes, Thomas (1651). The Matter, Form, and Power of a Common-Wealth Ecclesiasticall and Civil.

30. Holmes, Oliver (1897). "The Path of the Law," Volume 10, Harvard Law Review.

31. Katz, Daniel, and Michael Bommarito, Josh Blackman (2017). "A General Approach for Predicting the Behavior of the Supreme Court of the United States," April 12, 2017, PLOS ONE.

32. Kowalski, Robert, and Francesca Toni (1996). "Abstract Argumentation," AI-Law96.

33. Laswell, Harold (1955). "Current Studies of the Decision Process: Automation Creativity," Volume 8, Western Political Quarterly.

34. Libal, Tomer, and Alexander Steen (2019). "The NAI Suite: Drafting and Reasoning over Legal Texts," October 15, 2019, arXiv.

35. Lipton, Zachary (2017). "The Mythos of Model Interpretability," March 6, 2017, arXiv.

36. Martin, Andrew, and Kevin Quinn, Theodore Ruger, Pauline Kim (2004). "Competing Approaches to Predicting Supreme Court Decision Making," December 2014, Symposium on Forecasting U.S. Supreme Court Decisions.

37. McCarty, Thorne (1977). "Reflections on TAXMAN: An Experiment in Artificial Intelligence and Legal Reasoning," January 1977, Harvard Law Review.

38. Modgil, Sanjay, and Henry Prakken (2013). "The ASPIC+ Framework for Structured Argumentation: A Tutorial," December 16, 2013, Argument & Computation.

39. Mowbray, Andrew, and Philip Chung, Graham Greenleaf (2019). "Utilising AI in the Legal Assistance Sector," LegalAIIA Workshop, ICAIL, June 17, 2019, Montreal, Canada.

40. Parasuraman, Raja, and Thomas Sheridan, Christopher Wickens (2000). "A Model for Types and Levels of Human Interaction with Automation," May 2000, IEEE Transactions on Systems, Man, and Cybernetics.

41. Popple, James (1993). "SHYSTER: A Pragmatic Legal Expert System," Ph.D. Dissertation, Australian National University.

42. Prakken, Henry, and Giovanni Sartor (2015). "Law and Logic: A Review from an Argumentation Perspective," Volume 227, Artificial Intelligence.

43. Rissland, Edwina (1988). Artificial Intelligence and Legal Reasoning: A Discussion of the Field and Gardner's Book," Volume 9, AI Magazine.

44. Rissland, Edwina (1990). "Artificial Intelligence and Law: Stepping Stones to a Model of Legal Reasoning," Yale Law Journal.

45. Searle, John (1980). "Minds, Brains, and Programs," Volume 3, Behavioral and Brain Sciences.

46. Sunstein, Cass (2001). "Of Artificial Intelligence and Legal Reasoning," University of Chicago Law School, Public Law and Legal Theory Working Papers.

47. Sunstein, Cass, and Kevin Ashley, Karl Branting, Howard Margolis (2001). "Legal Reasoning and Artificial Intelligence: How Computers 'Think' Like Lawyers," Symposium: Legal Reasoning and Artificial Intelligence, University of Chicago Law School Roundtable.

48. Surden, Harry (2014). "Machine Learning and Law," Washington Law Review.

49. Surden, Harry (2019). "Artificial Intelligence and Law: An Overview," Summer 2019, Georgia State University Law Review.

50. Valente, Andre, and Joost Breuker (1996). "A Functional Ontology of Law," Artificial Intelligence and Law.

51. Waltl, Bernhard, and Roland Vogl (2018). "Explainable Artificial Intelligence: The New Frontier in Legal Informatics," February 2018, Jusletter IT 22, Stanford Center for Legal Informatics, Stanford University.

52. Wittgenstein, Ludwig (1953). Philosophical Investigations. Blackwell Publishing.

APPENDIX B
SUPPLEMENTAL FIGURES AND CHARTS

For the convenience of viewing, supplemental figures and charts related to the topics discussed are shown on the next pages

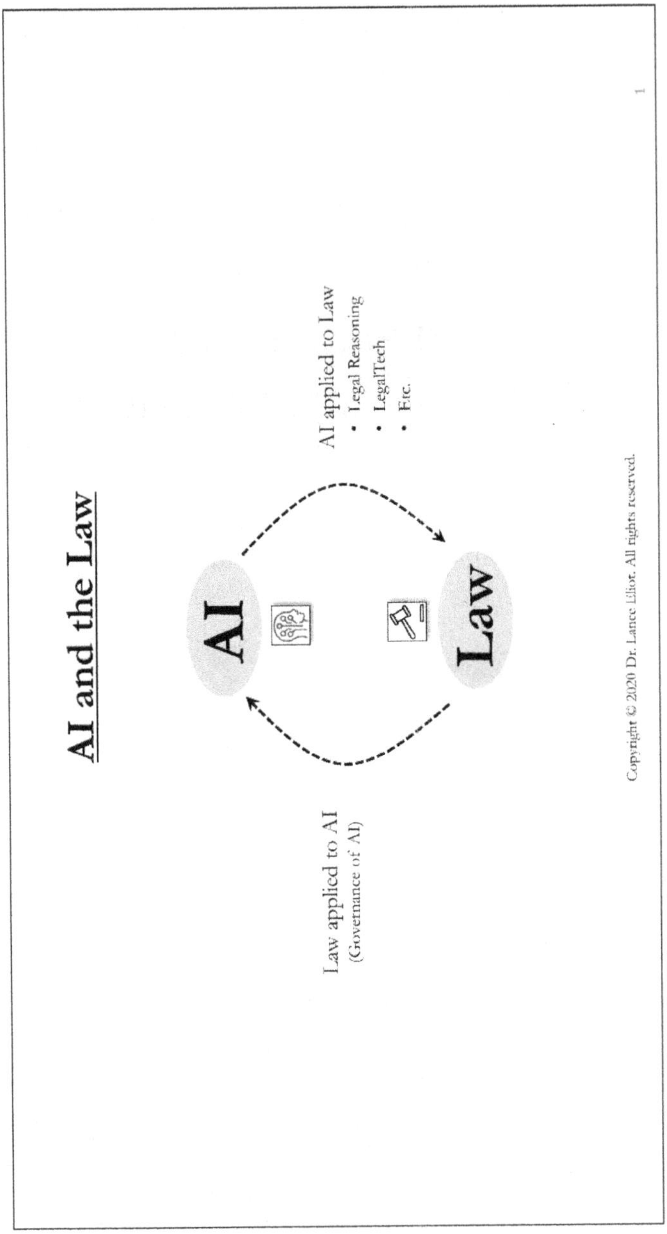
AI and the Law
AI
Law
AI applied to Law
• Legal Reasoning
• LegalTech
• Etc.
Law applied to AI
(Governance of AI)
Copyright © 2020 Dr. Lance Eliot. All rights reserved.
1

Figure 1

AI & Law: Levels of Autonomy For AI Legal Reasoning (AILR)

Level	Descriptor	Examples	Automation	Status
0	No Automation	Manual, paper-based (no automation)	None	De Facto - In Use
1	Simple Assistance Automation	Word Processing, XLS, online legal docs, etc.	Legal Assist	Widely In Use
2	Advanced Assistance Automation	Query-style NLP, ML for case prediction, etc.	Legal Assist	Some In Use
3	Semi-Autonomous Automation	KBS & ML/DL for legal reasoning & analysis, etc.	Legal Assist	Primarily Prototypes & Research Based
4	AILR Domain Autonomous	Versed only in a specific legal domain	Legal Advisor (law fluent)	None As Yet
5	AILR Fully Autonomous	Versatile within and across all legal domains	Legal Advisor (law fluent)	None As Yet
6	AILR Superhuman Autonomous	Exceeds human-based legal reasoning	Supra Legal Advisor	Indeterminate

Figure 1: AI & Law - Autonomous Levels by Rows

Source Author: Dr. Lance B. Eliot

V1.3

Figure 2

AI & Law: Levels of Autonomy For AI Legal Reasoning (AILR)

	Level 0	Level 1	Level 2	Level 3	Level 4	Level 5	Level 6
Descriptor	No Automation	Simple Assistance Automation	Advanced Assistance Automation	Semi-Autonomous Automation	AILR Domain Autonomous	AILR Fully Autonomous	AILR Superhuman Autonomous
Examples	Manual, paper-based (no automation)	Word Processing, XLS, online legal docs, etc.	Query-style NLP, ML for case prediction, etc.	KBS & ML/DL for legal reasoning & analysis, etc.	Versed only in a specific legal domain	Versatile within and across all legal domains	Exceeds human-based legal reasoning
Automation	None	Legal Assist	Legal Assist	Legal Assist	Legal Advisor (law fluent)	Legal Advisor (law fluent)	Supra Legal Advisor
Status	De Facto – In Use	Widely In Use	Some In Use	Primarily Prototypes & Research-based	None As Yet	None As Yet	Indeterminate

Figure 2: AI & Law - Autonomous Levels by Columns

Source Author: Dr. Lance B. Eliot

V1.3

Figure 3

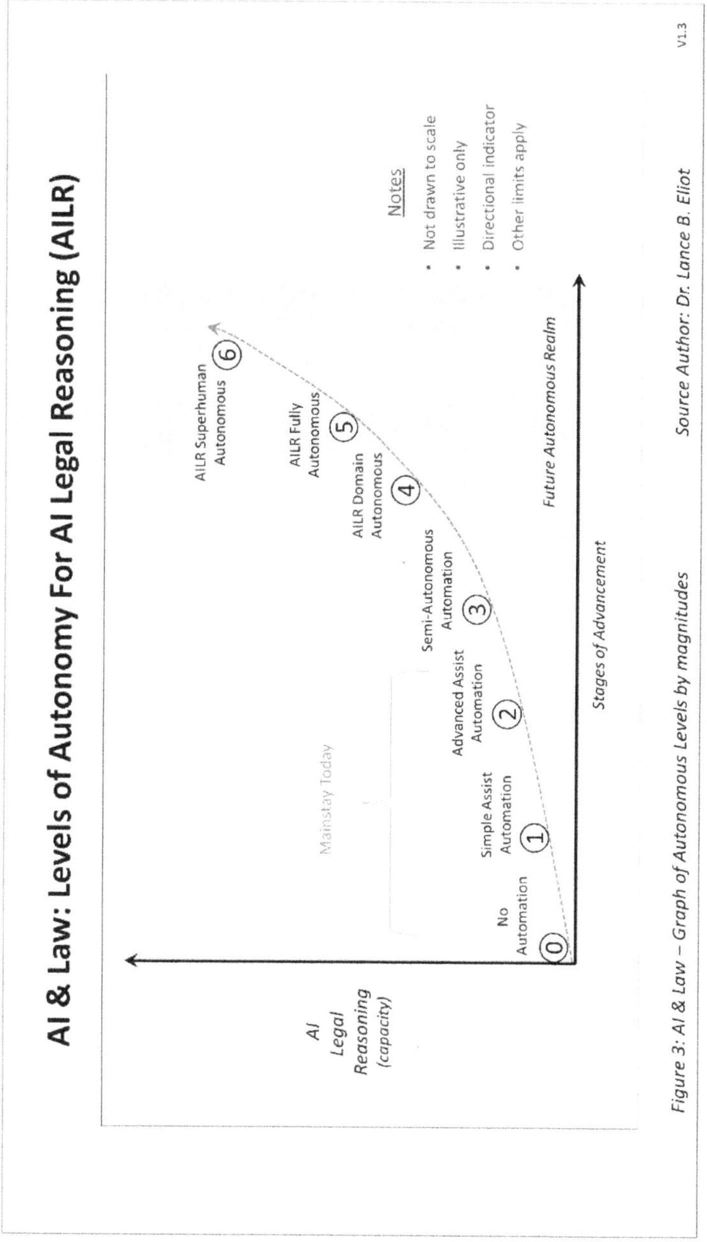
AI & Law: Levels of Autonomy For AI Legal Reasoning (AILR)
AI Legal Reasoning (capacity)
0 No Automation
1 Simple Assist Automation
2 Advanced Assist Automation
3 Semi-Autonomous Automation
4 AILR Domain Autonomous
5 AILR Fully Autonomous
6 AILR Superhuman Autonomous
Mainstay Today
Stages of Advancement
Future Autonomous Realm
Notes
Not drawn to scale
Illustrative only
Directional indicator
Other limits apply
V1.3
Figure 3: AI & Law – Graph of Autonomous Levels by magnitudes
Source Author: Dr. Lance B. Eliot

Figure 4

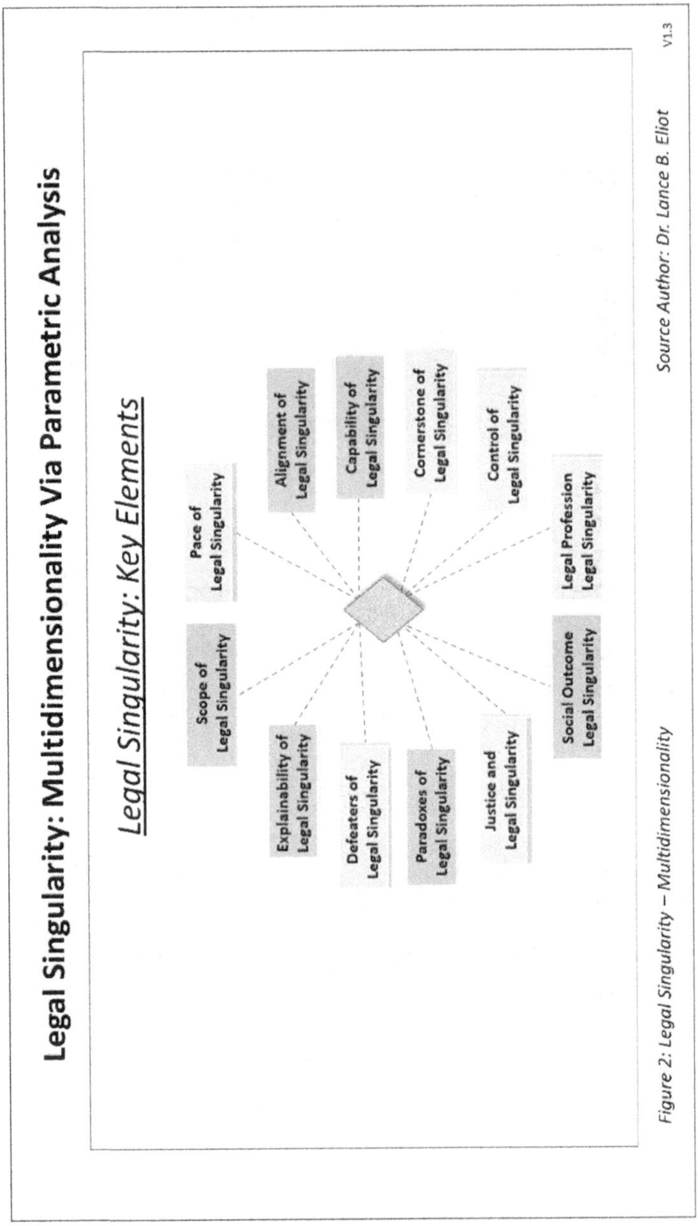
Legal Singularity: Multidimensionality Via Parametric Analysis
Legal Singularity: Key Elements
Scope of Legal Singularity
Pace of Legal Singularity
Explainability of Legal Singularity
Alignment of Legal Singularity
Defeaters of Legal Singularity
Capability of Legal Singularity
Paradoxes of Legal Singularity
Cornerstone of Legal Singularity
Justice and Legal Singularity
Control of Legal Singularity
Social Outcome Legal Singularity
Legal Profession Legal Singularity
Figure 2: Legal Singularity – Multidimensionality
Source Author: Dr. Lance B. Eliot
V1.3

Figure 5

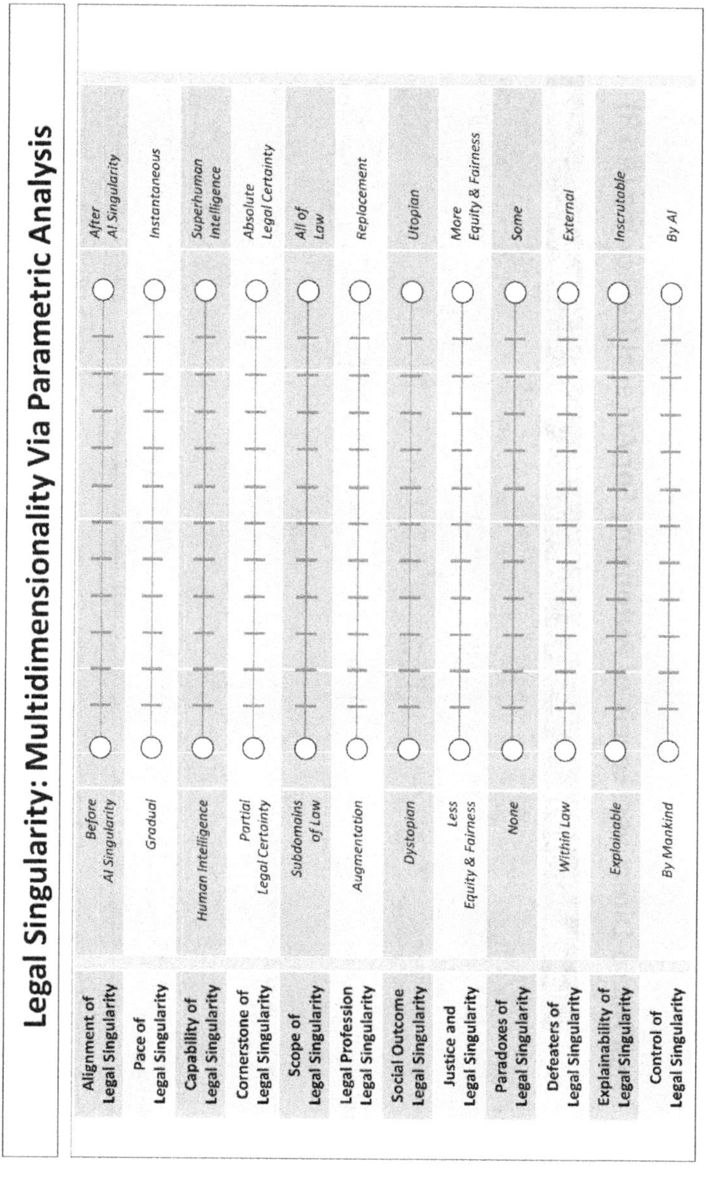

Figure 3: Legal Singularity Multidimensionality and Parametric Analysis

Source Author: Dr. Lance B. Eliot

Figure 6

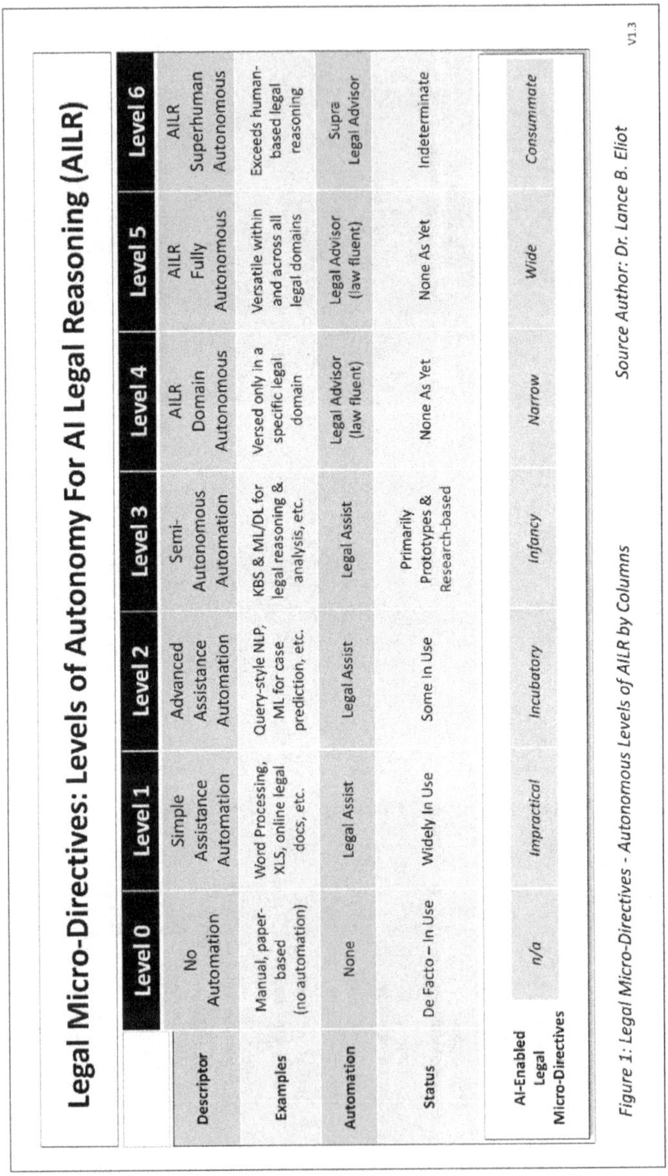

Legal Micro-Directives: Levels of Autonomy For AI Legal Reasoning (AILR)

	Level 0	Level 1	Level 2	Level 3	Level 4	Level 5	Level 6
Descriptor	No Automation	Simple Assistance Automation	Advanced Assistance Automation	Semi-Autonomous Automation	AILR Domain Autonomous	AILR Fully Autonomous	AILR Superhuman Autonomous
Examples	Manual, paper-based (no automation)	Word Processing, XLS, online legal docs, etc.	Query-style NLP, ML for case prediction, etc.	KBS & ML/DL for legal reasoning & analysis, etc.	Versed only in a specific legal domain	Versatile within and across all legal domains	Exceeds human-based legal reasoning
Automation	None	Legal Assist	Legal Assist	Legal Assist	Legal Advisor (law fluent)	Legal Advisor (law fluent)	Supra Legal Advisor
Status	De Facto – In Use	Widely In Use	Some In Use	Primarily Prototypes & Research-based	None As Yet	None As Yet	Indeterminate
AI-Enabled Legal Micro-Directives	*n/a*	*Impractical*	*Incubatory*	*Infancy*	*Narrow*	*Wide*	*Consummate*

Figure 1: Legal Micro-Directives - Autonomous Levels of AILR by Columns

Source Author: Dr. Lance B. Eliot

V1.3

Figure 7

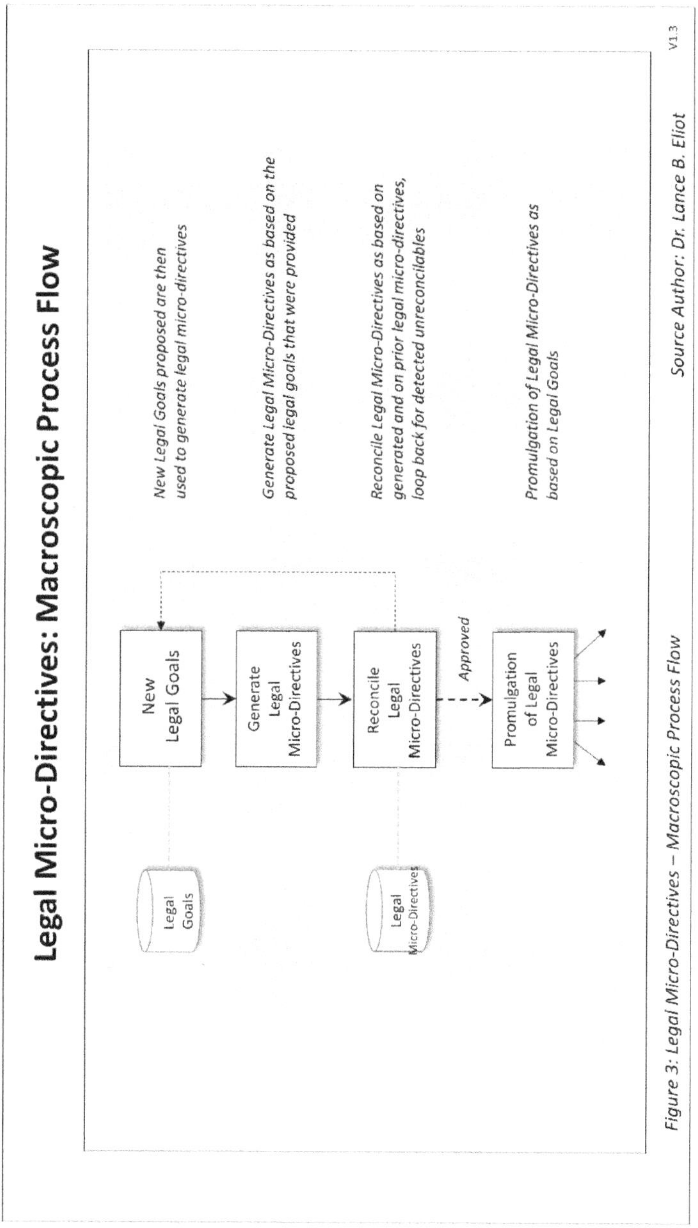
Legal Micro-Directives: Macroscopic Process Flow
Legal Goals
Legal Micro-Directives
New Legal Goals
Generate Legal Micro-Directives
Reconcile Legal Micro-Directives
Approved
Promulgation of Legal Micro-Directives
New Legal Goals proposed are then used to generate legal micro-directives
Generate Legal Micro-Directives as based on the proposed legal goals that were provided
Reconcile Legal Micro-Directives as based on generated and on prior legal micro-directives, loop back for detected unreconcilables
Promulgation of Legal Micro-Directives as based on Legal Goals
Figure 3: Legal Micro-Directives – Macroscopic Process Flow
Source Author: Dr. Lance B. Eliot
V1.3

Figure 8

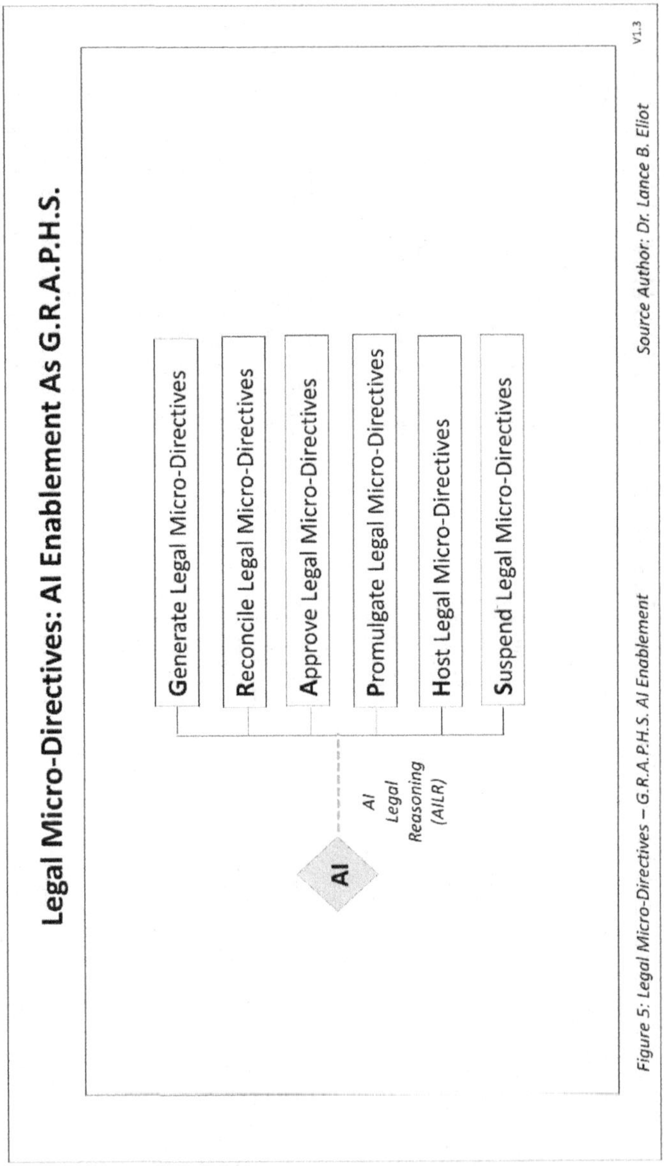
Legal Micro-Directives: AI Enablement As G.R.A.P.H.S.
AI
AI
Legal
Reasoning
(AILR)
Generate Legal Micro-Directives
Reconcile Legal Micro-Directives
Approve Legal Micro-Directives
Promulgate Legal Micro-Directives
Host Legal Micro-Directives
Suspend Legal Micro-Directives
Figure 5: Legal Micro-Directives – G.R.A.P.H.S. AI Enablement
Source Author: Dr. Lance B. Eliot
V1.3

Figure 9

Legal Argumentation: Levels of Autonomy For AI Legal Reasoning (AILR)

	Level 0	Level 1	Level 2	Level 3	Level 4	Level 5	Level 6
Descriptor	No Automation	Simple Assistance Automation	Advanced Assistance Automation	Semi-Autonomous Automation	AILR Domain Autonomous	AILR Fully Autonomous	AILR Superhuman Autonomous
Examples	Manual, paper-based (no automation)	Word Processing, XLS, online legal docs, etc.	Query-style NLP, ML for case prediction, etc.	KBS & ML/DL for legal reasoning & analysis, etc.	Versed only in a specific legal domain	Versatile within and across all legal domains	Exceeds human-based legal reasoning
Automation	None	Legal Assist	Legal Assist	Legal Assist	Legal Advisor (law fluent)	Legal Advisor (law fluent)	Supra Legal Advisor
Status	De Facto – In Use	Widely In Use	Some In Use	Primarily Prototypes & Research-based	None As Yet	None As Yet	Indeterminate
AI-Enabled Legal Argumentation	*n/a*	*Mechanistic (Low)*	*Mechanistic (High)*	*Expressive*	*Domain Fluency*	*Full Fluency*	*Meta-Fluency*

Figure 7: AI Legal Argumentation (AILA) - Autonomous Levels of AILR by Columns

Source Author: Dr. Lance B. Eliot

V1.3

Figure 10

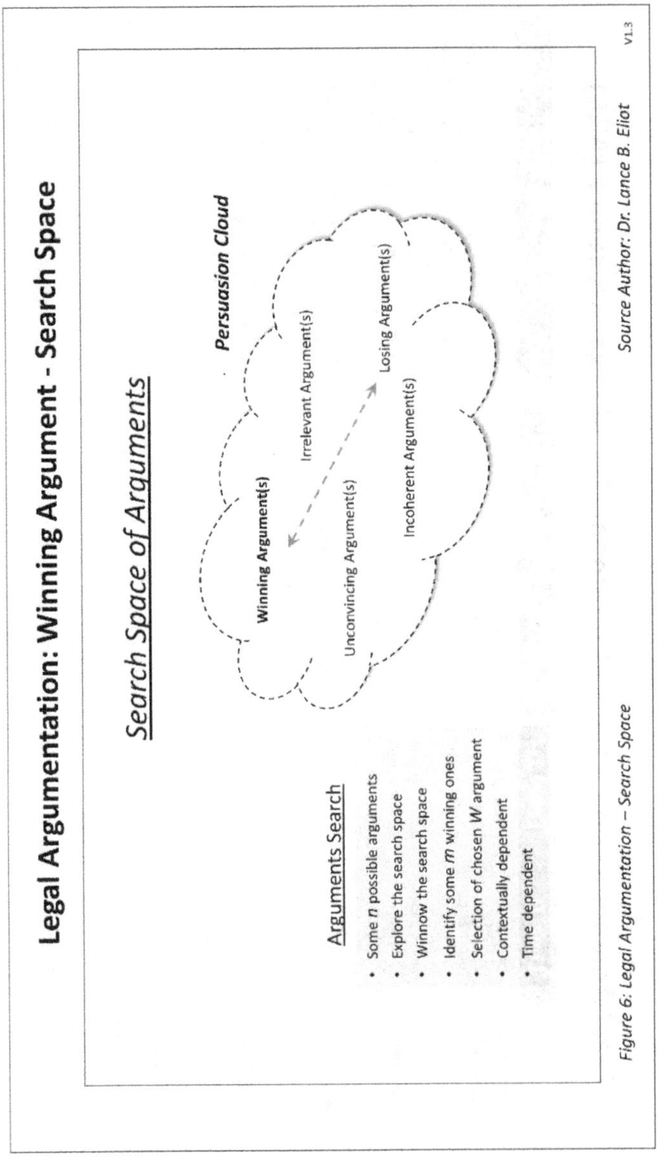

Legal Argumentation: Winning Argument - Search Space
Search Space of Arguments
Persuasion Cloud
Winning Argument(s)
Irrelevant Argument(s)
Losing Argument(s)
Unconvincing Argument(s)
Incoherent Argument(s)
Arguments Search
• Some n possible arguments
• Explore the search space
• Winnow the search space
• Identify some m winning ones
• Selection of chosen W argument
• Contextually dependent
• Time dependent
Figure 6: Legal Argumentation – Search Space
Source Author: Dr. Lance B. Eliot
V1.3

Figure 11

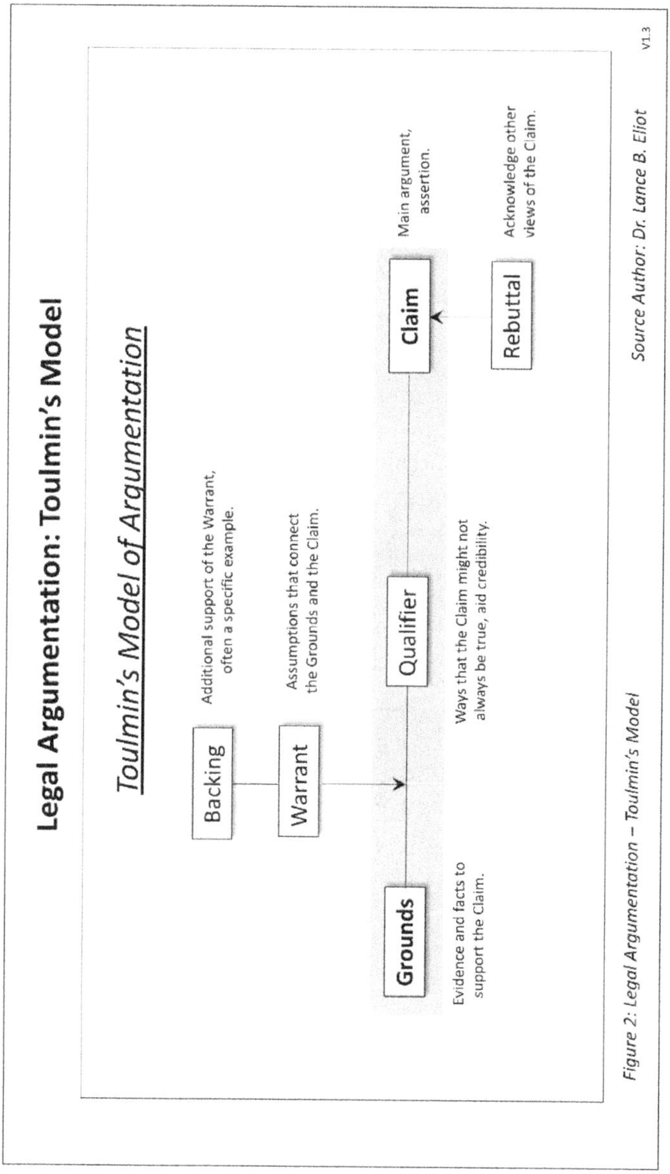
Legal Argumentation: Toulmin's Model
Toulmin's Model of Argumentation
Backing
Additional support of the Warrant, often a specific example.
Warrant
Assumptions that connect the Grounds and the Claim.
Grounds
Evidence and facts to support the Claim.
Qualifier
Ways that the Claim might not always be true, aid credibility.
Claim
Main argument, assertion.
Rebuttal
Acknowledge other views of the Claim.
Figure 2: Legal Argumentation – Toulmin's Model
Source Author: Dr. Lance B. Eliot
V1.3

Figure 12

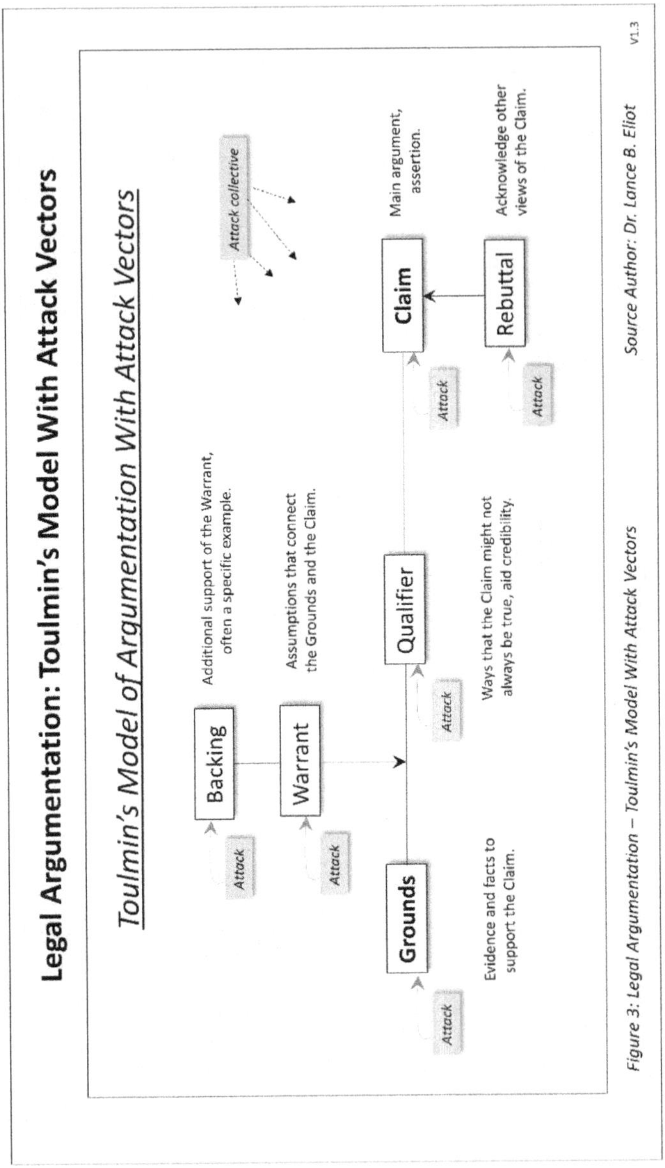
Legal Argumentation: Toulmin's Model With Attack Vectors
Toulmin's Model of Argumentation With Attack Vectors
Attack collective
Backing
Attack
Additional support of the Warrant, often a specific example.
Warrant
Attack
Assumptions that connect the Grounds and the Claim.
Grounds
Attack
Evidence and facts to support the Claim.
Qualifier
Attack
Ways that the Claim might not always be true, aid credibility.
Claim
Attack
Main argument, assertion.
Rebuttal
Attack
Acknowledge other views of the Claim.
Figure 3: Legal Argumentation – Toulmin's Model With Attack Vectors
Source Author: Dr. Lance B. Eliot
V1.3

Figure 13

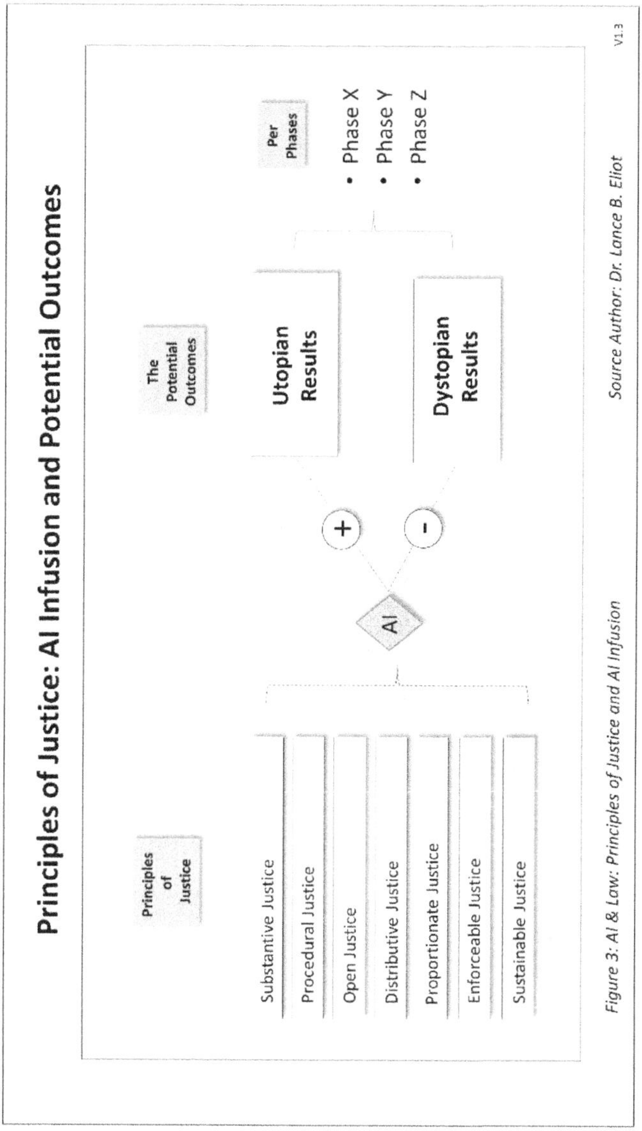
Principles of Justice: AI Infusion and Potential Outcomes
Principles of Justice
The Potential Outcomes
Per Phases
Substantive Justice
Procedural Justice
Open Justice
Distributive Justice
Proportionate Justice
Enforceable Justice
Sustainable Justice
AI
+
-
Utopian Results
Dystopian Results
• Phase X
• Phase Y
• Phase Z
Figure 3: AI & Law: Principles of Justice and AI Infusion
Source Author: Dr. Lance B. Eliot
V1.3

Figure 14

Principles of Justice and Autonomous Levels of AI Legal Reasoning (AILR)

	Level 0	Level 1	Level 2	Level 3	Level 4	Level 5	Level 6
Descriptor	No Automation	Simple Assistance Automation	Advanced Assistance Automation	Semi-Autonomous Automation	AILR Domain Autonomous	AILR Fully Autonomous	AILR Superhuman Autonomous
Substantive Justice	*Traditional*	*Traditional*	*Traditional*	Emerging	Phase X Impacts	Phase Y Impacts	Phase Z Impacts
Procedural Justice	*Traditional*	*Traditional*	*Traditional*	Emerging	Phase X Impacts	Phase Y Impacts	Phase Z Impacts
Open Justice	*Traditional*	*Traditional*	*Traditional*	Emerging	Phase X Impacts	Phase Y Impacts	Phase Z Impacts
Distributive Justice	*Traditional*	*Traditional*	*Traditional*	Emerging	Phase X Impacts	Phase Y Impacts	Phase Z Impacts
Proportionate Justice	*Traditional*	*Traditional*	*Traditional*	Emerging	Phase X Impacts	Phase Y Impacts	Phase Z Impacts
Enforceable Justice	*Traditional*	*Traditional*	*Traditional*	Emerging	Phase X Impacts	Phase Y Impacts	Phase Z Impacts
Sustainable Justice	*Traditional*	*Traditional*	*Traditional*	Emerging	Phase X Impacts	Phase Y Impacts	Phase Z Impacts

Figure 1: AI & Law – Principles of Justice and LoA AILR by Columns

Source Author: Dr. Lance B. Eliot

V1.3

Figure 15

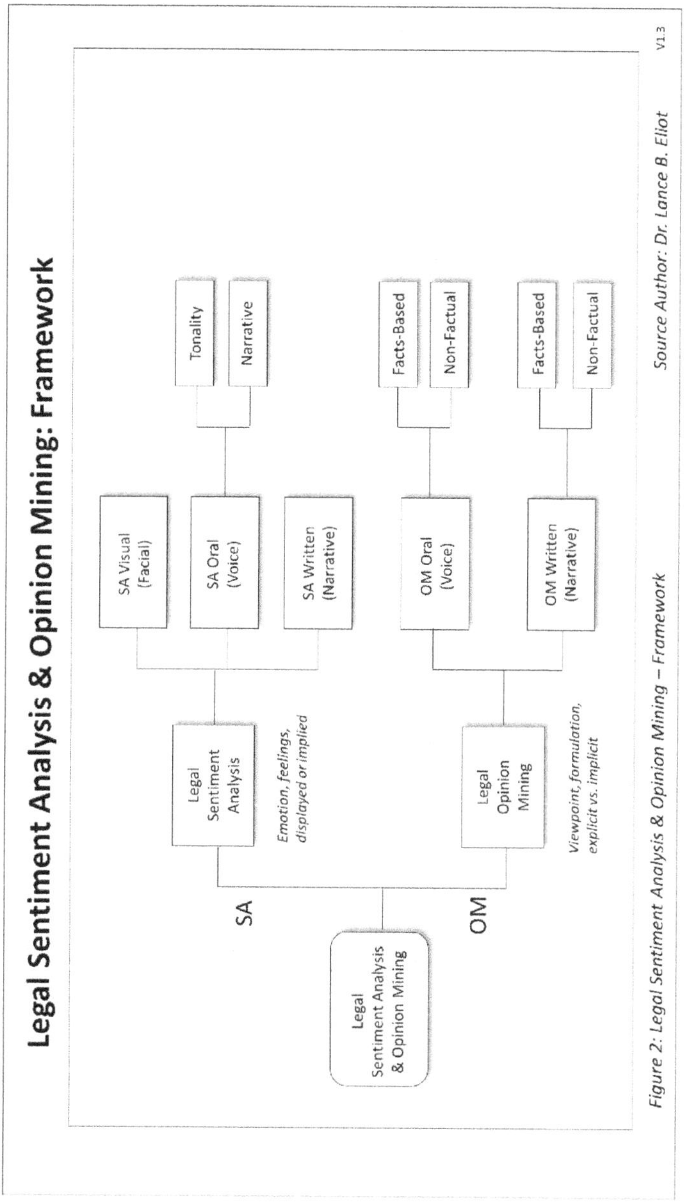
Legal Sentiment Analysis & Opinion Mining: Framework
Legal Sentiment Analysis & Opinion Mining
SA
OM
Legal Sentiment Analysis
Emotion, feelings, displayed or implied
Legal Opinion Mining
Viewpoint, formulation, explicit vs. implicit
SA Visual (Facial)
SA Oral (Voice)
SA Written (Narrative)
OM Oral (Voice)
OM Written (Narrative)
Tonality
Narrative
Facts-Based
Non-Factual
Facts-Based
Non-Factual
Figure 2: Legal Sentiment Analysis & Opinion Mining – Framework
Source Author: Dr. Lance B. Eliot
V1.3

Figure 16

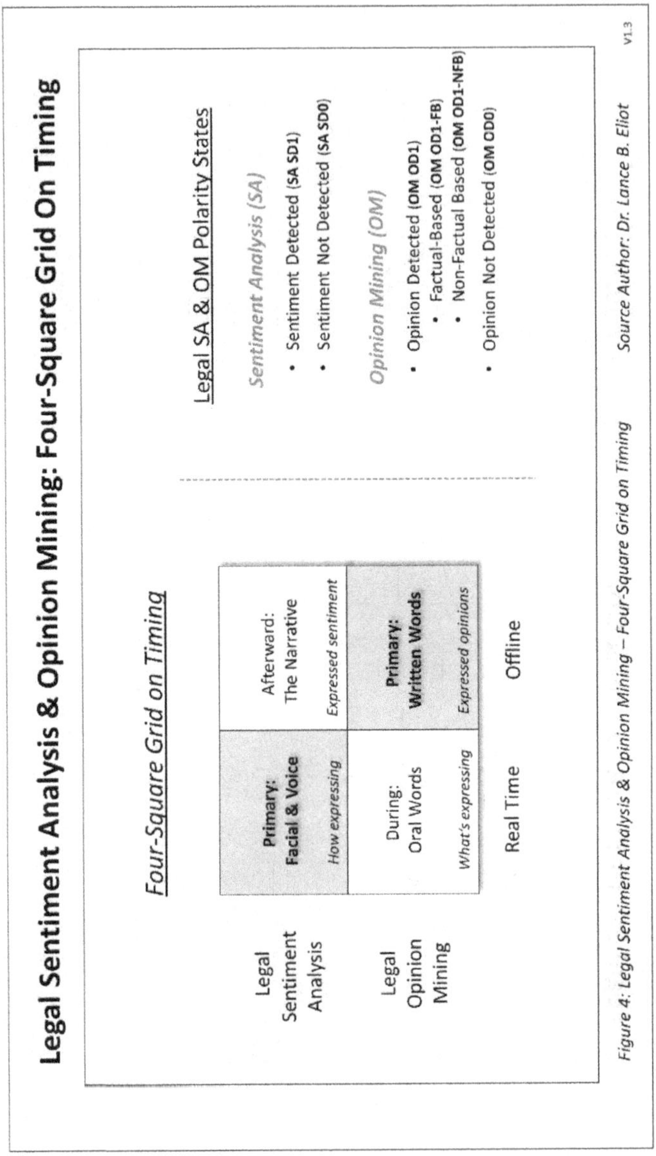

Legal Sentiment Analysis & Opinion Mining: Four-Square Grid On Timing
Four-Square Grid on Timing
Legal Sentiment Analysis
Legal Opinion Mining
Primary: Facial & Voice
How expressing
Afterward: The Narrative
Expressed sentiment
During: Oral Words
What's expressing
Primary: Written Words
Expressed opinions
Real Time
Offline
Legal SA & OM Polarity States
Sentiment Analysis (SA)
Sentiment Detected (SA SD1)
Sentiment Not Detected (SA SD0)
Opinion Mining (OM)
Opinion Detected (OM OD1)
Factual-Based (OM OD1-FB)
Non-Factual Based (OM OD1-NFB)
Opinion Not Detected (OM OD0)
Figure 4: Legal Sentiment Analysis & Opinion Mining – Four-Square Grid on Timing
Source Author: Dr. Lance B. Eliot
V1.3

Figure 17

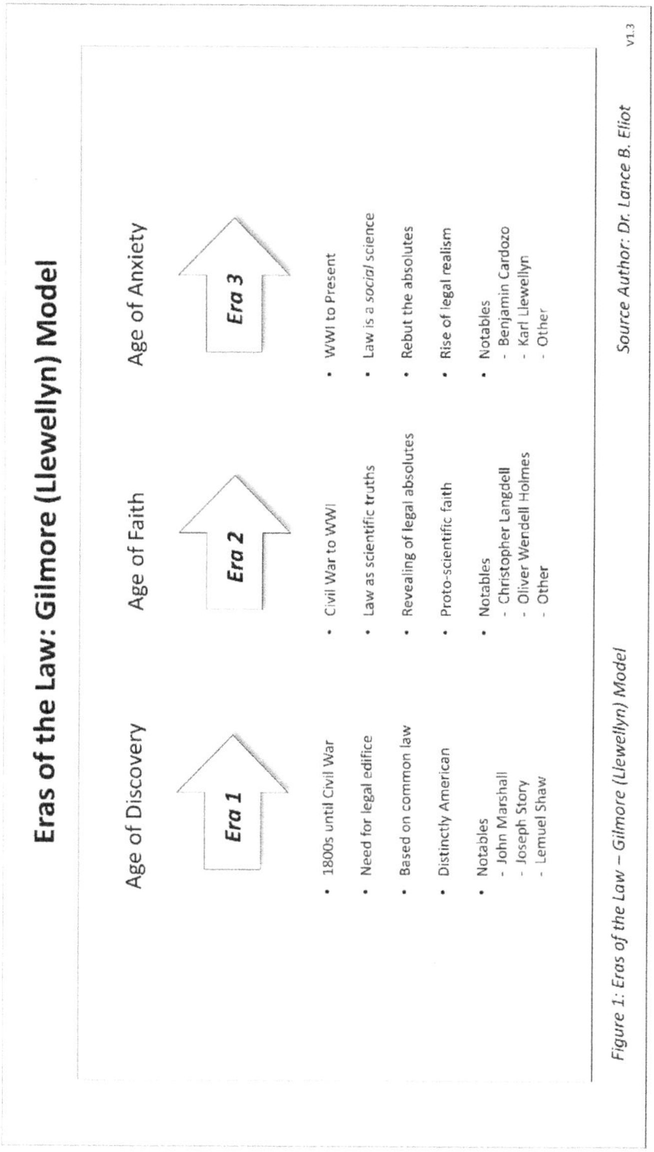
Eras of the Law: Gilmore (Llewellyn) Model
Age of Discovery
Era 1
1800s until Civil War
Need for legal edifice
Based on common law
Distinctly American
Notables
- John Marshall
- Joseph Story
- Lemuel Shaw
Age of Faith
Era 2
Civil War to WWI
Law as scientific truths
Revealing of legal absolutes
Proto-scientific faith
Notables
- Christopher Langdell
- Oliver Wendell Holmes
- Other
Age of Anxiety
Era 3
WWI to Present
Law is a social science
Rebut the absolutes
Rise of legal realism
Notables
- Benjamin Cardozo
- Karl Llewellyn
- Other
Figure 1: Eras of the Law – Gilmore (Llewellyn) Model
Source Author: Dr. Lance B. Eliot
v1.3

Figure 18

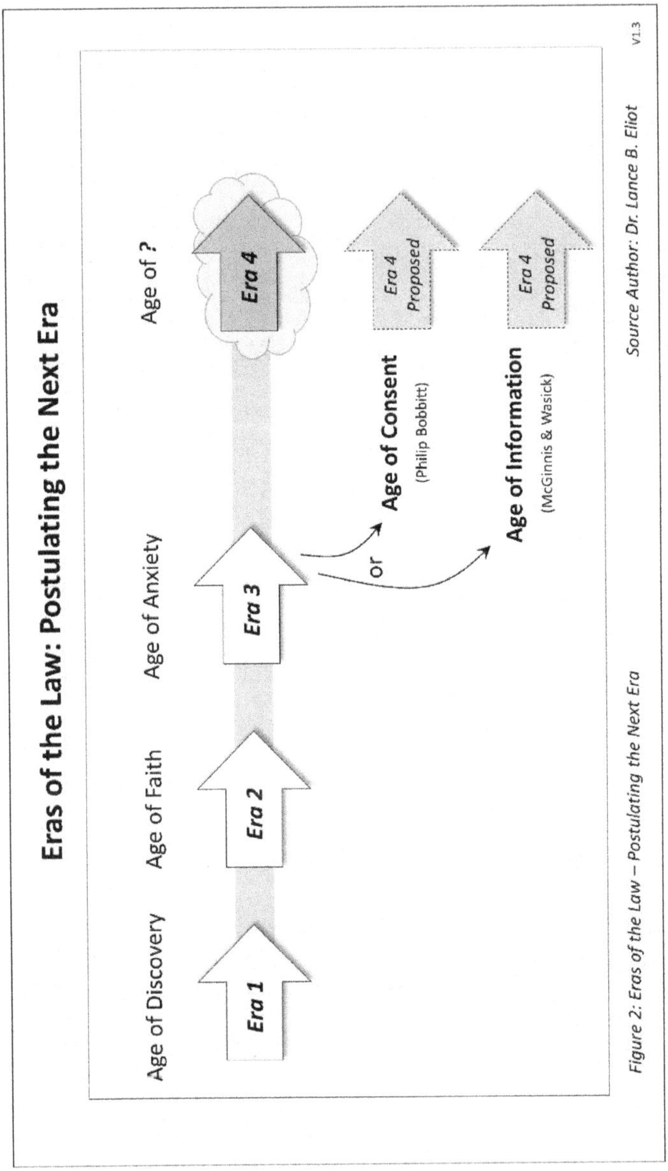
Eras of the Law: Postulating the Next Era
Age of Discovery
Age of Faith
Age of Anxiety
Age of ?
Era 1
Era 2
Era 3
Era 4
or
Age of Consent
(Philip Bobbitt)
Era 4 Proposed
Age of Information
(McGinnis & Wasick)
Era 4 Proposed
Figure 2: Eras of the Law – Postulating the Next Era
Source Author: Dr. Lance B. Eliot
V1.3

Figure 19

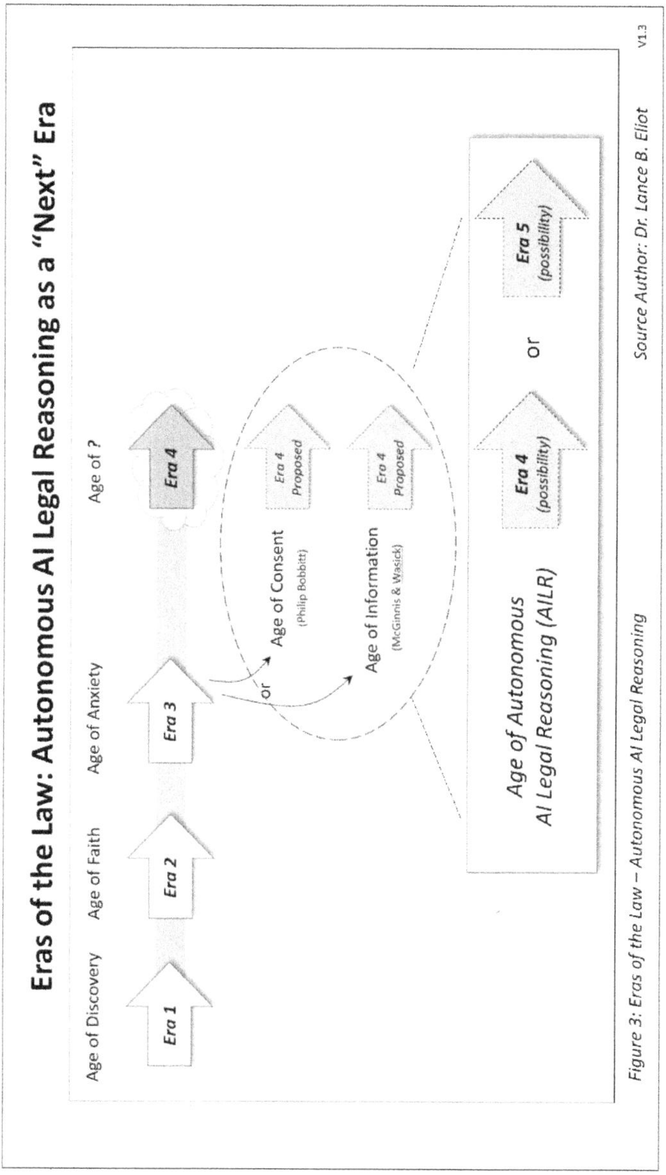
Eras of the Law: Autonomous AI Legal Reasoning as a "Next" Era
Age of Discovery
Age of Faith
Age of Anxiety
Age of ?
Era 1
Era 2
Era 3
Era 4
or
Age of Consent
(Philip Bobbitt)
Age of Information
(McGinnis & Wasick)
Era 4 Proposed
Era 4 Proposed
Age of Autonomous
AI Legal Reasoning (AILR)
Era 4
(possibility)
or
Era 5
(possibility)
Figure 3: Eras of the Law – Autonomous AI Legal Reasoning
Source Author: Dr. Lance B. Eliot
V1.3

Figure 20

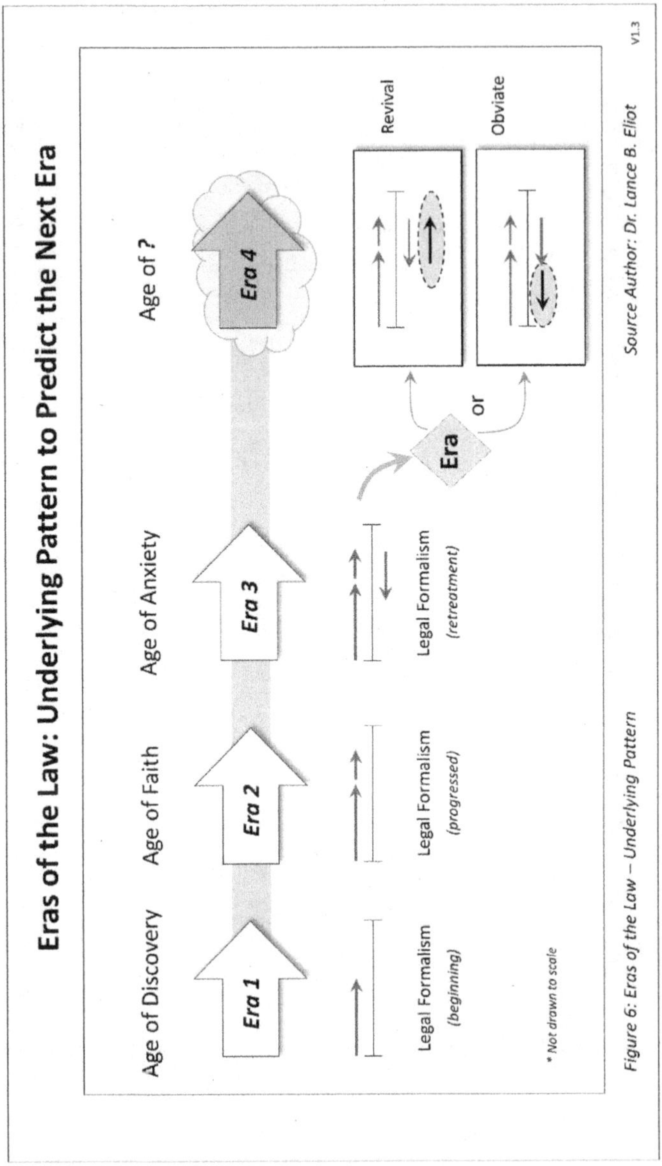
Eras of the Law: Underlying Pattern to Predict the Next Era
Age of Discovery
Age of Faith
Age of Anxiety
Age of ?
Era 1
Era 2
Era 3
Era 4
Legal Formalism
(beginning)
Legal Formalism
(progressed)
Legal Formalism
(retreatment)
Era
or
Revival
Obviate
* Not drawn to scale
Figure 6: Eras of the Law – Underlying Pattern
Source Author: Dr. Lance B. Eliot
V1.3

Figure 21

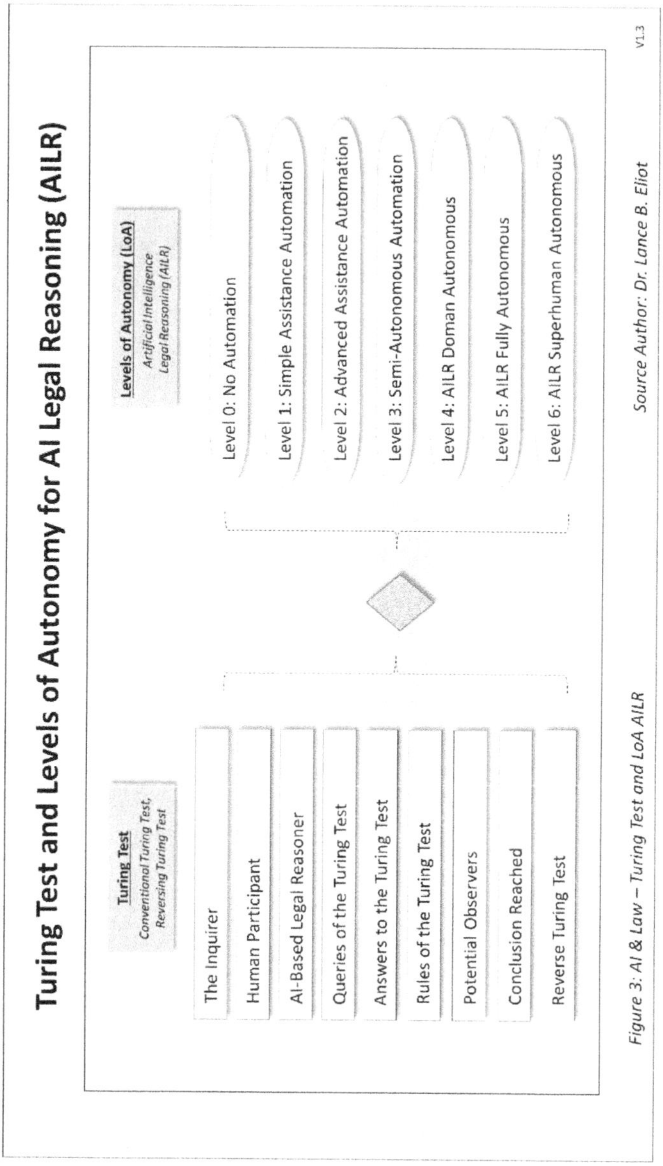

Figure 3: AI & Law – Turing Test and LoA AILR

Figure 22

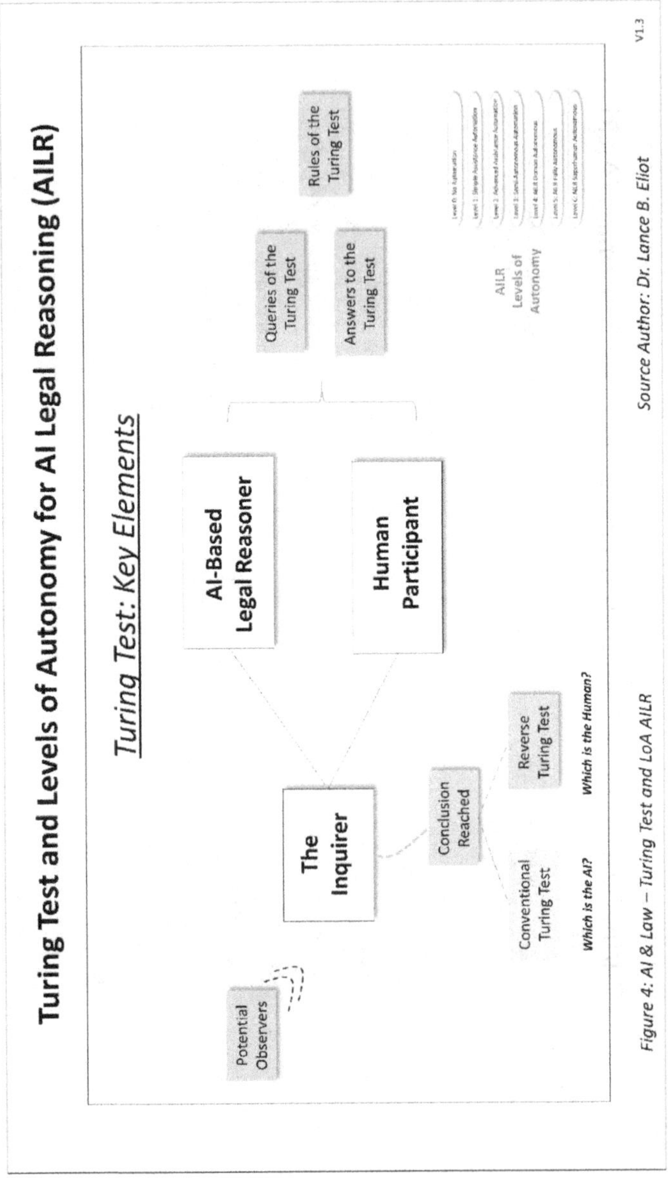
Turing Test and Levels of Autonomy for AI Legal Reasoning (AILR)
Turing Test: Key Elements
Potential Observers
The Inquirer
AI-Based Legal Reasoner
Human Participant
Queries of the Turing Test
Answers to the Turing Test
Rules of the Turing Test
Conclusion Reached
Conventional Turing Test
Reverse Turing Test
Which is the AI?
Which is the Human?
AILR Levels of Autonomy
V1.3
Figure 4: AI & Law – Turing Test and LoA AILR
Source Author: Dr. Lance B. Eliot

Figure 23

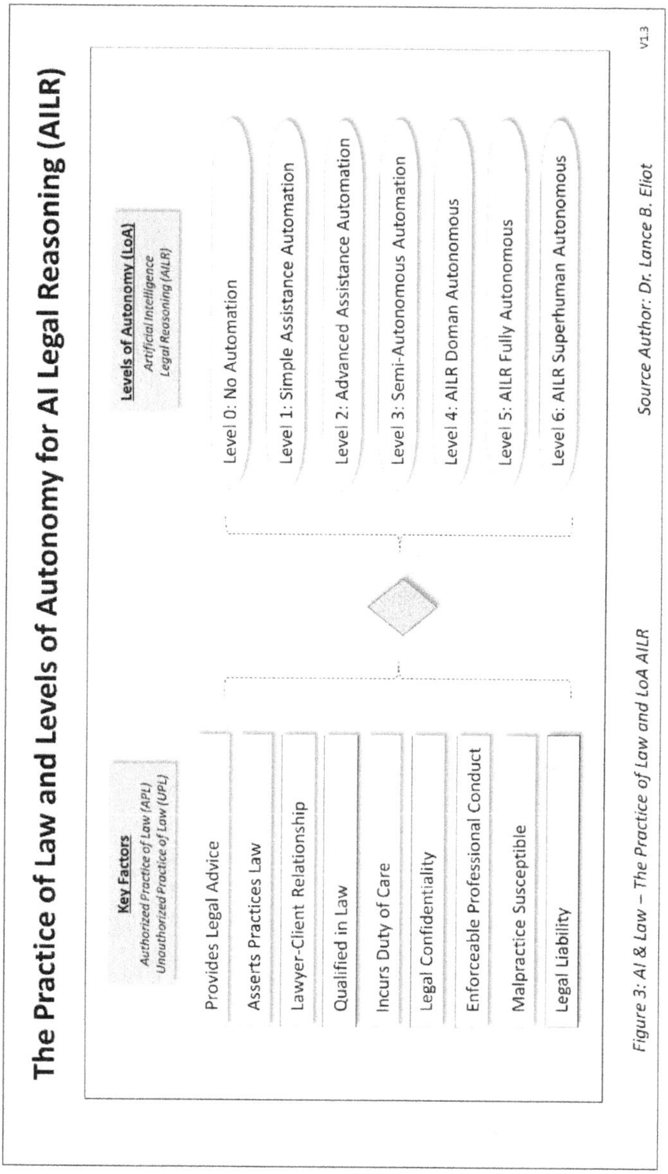
The Practice of Law and Levels of Autonomy for AI Legal Reasoning (AILR)
Key Factors
Authorized Practice of Law (APL)
Unauthorized Practice of Law (UPL)
Provides Legal Advice
Asserts Practices Law
Lawyer-Client Relationship
Qualified in Law
Incurs Duty of Care
Legal Confidentiality
Enforceable Professional Conduct
Malpractice Susceptible
Legal Liability
Levels of Autonomy (LoA)
Artificial Intelligence
Legal Reasoning (AILR)
Level 0: No Automation
Level 1: Simple Assistance Automation
Level 2: Advanced Assistance Automation
Level 3: Semi-Autonomous Automation
Level 4: AILR Doman Autonomous
Level 5: AILR Fully Autonomous
Level 6: AILR Superhuman Autonomous
Figure 3: AI & Law – The Practice of Law and LoA AILR
Source Author: Dr. Lance B. Eliot
V1.3

Figure 24

The Practice of Law and Autonomous Levels of AI Legal Reasoning (AILR)

Descriptor	Level 0 No Automation	Level 1 Simple Assistance Automation	Level 2 Advanced Assistance Automation	Level 3 Semi-Autonomous Automation	Level 4 AILR Domain Autonomous	Level 5 AILR Fully Autonomous	Level 6 AILR Superhuman Autonomous
Provides Legal Advice	n/a	No	Maybe	Yes	Yes	Yes	Yes Plus
Asserts Practices Law	n/a	No	No	No	Yes	Yes	Yes Plus
Lawyer-Client Relationship	n/a	No	No	No	Partial	Yes	Yes
Qualified in Law	n/a	No	No	Minimal	Partial	Yes	Yes Plus
Incurs Duty of Care	n/a	No	No	No	Likely	Yes	Yes
Legal Confidentiality	n/a	No	No	No	Likely	Yes	Yes
Enforceable Prof Conduct	n/a	No	No	No	Likely	Yes	Yes
Malpractice Susceptible	n/a	No	No	No	Likely	Yes	Yes
Legal Liability	n/a	No	Maybe	Likely	Likely	Yes	Yes

Strawman Variant

Figure 1: AI & Law – The Practice of Law and LoA AILR by Columns

Source Author: Dr. Lance B. Eliot

V1.3

Figure 25

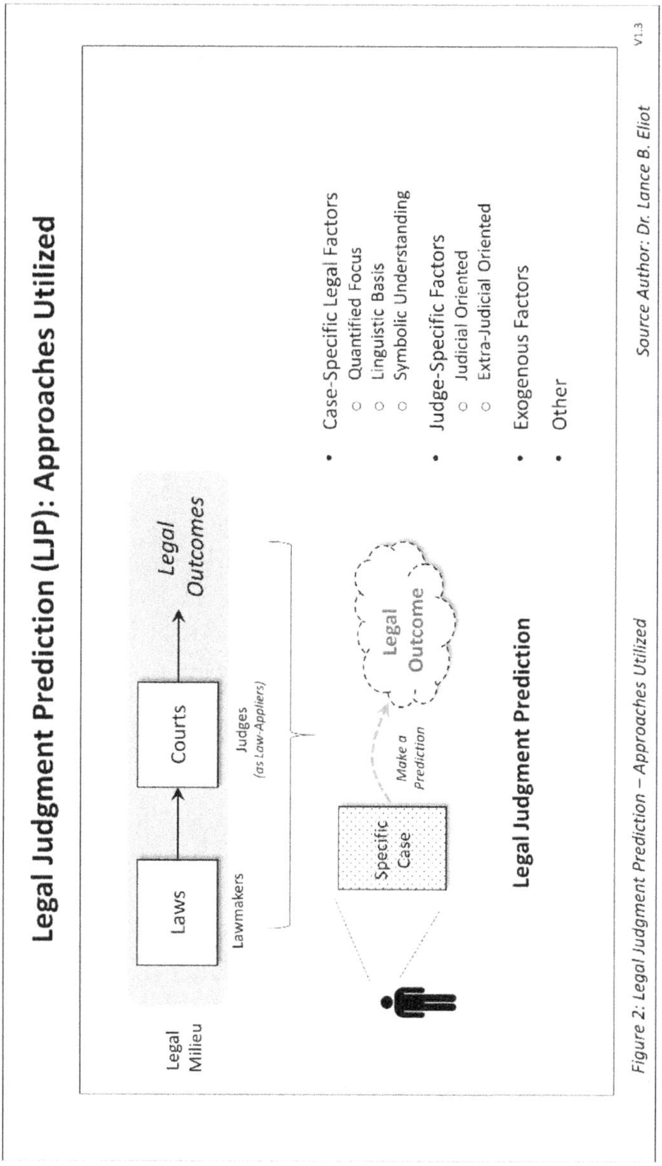
Legal Judgment Prediction (LJP): Approaches Utilized
Legal Milieu
Laws
Courts
Legal Outcomes
Lawmakers
Judges
(as Law-Appliers)
Specific Case
Make a Prediction
Legal Outcome
Legal Judgment Prediction
Case-Specific Legal Factors
Quantified Focus
Linguistic Basis
Symbolic Understanding
Judge-Specific Factors
Judicial Oriented
Extra-Judicial Oriented
Exogenous Factors
Other
Figure 2: Legal Judgment Prediction – Approaches Utilized
Source Author: Dr. Lance B. Eliot
V1.3

Figure 26

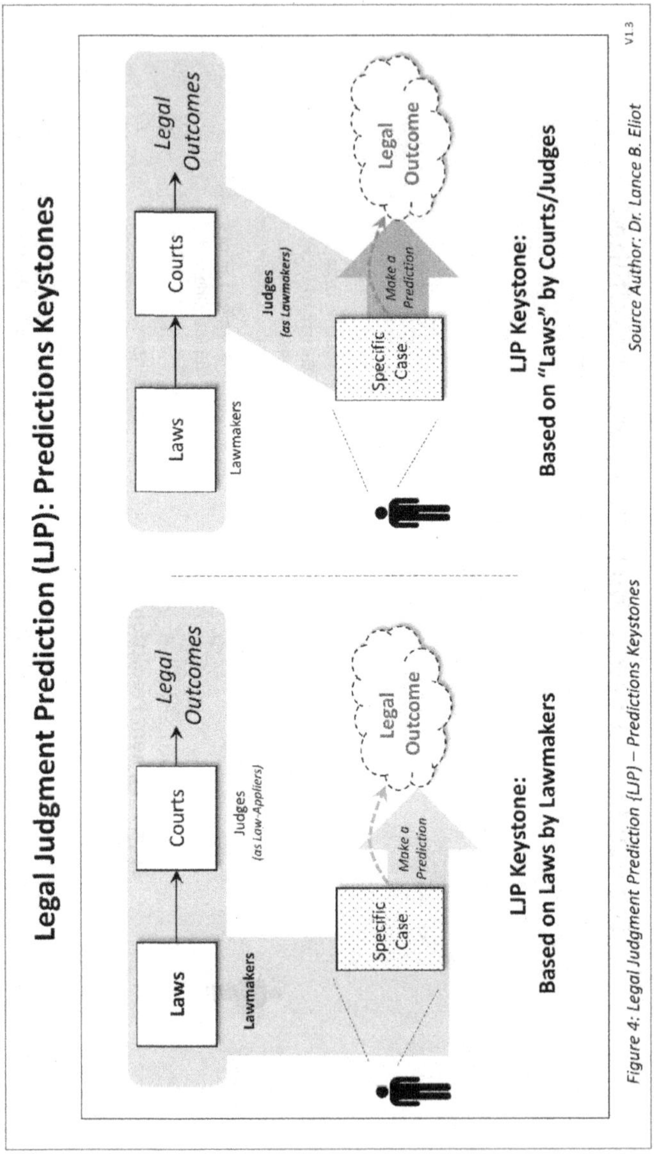
Legal Judgment Prediction (LJP): Predictions Keystones
Laws
Courts
Legal Outcomes
Lawmakers
Judges (as Law-Appliers)
Specific Case
Make a Prediction
Legal Outcome
LJP Keystone: Based on Laws by Lawmakers
Laws
Courts
Legal Outcomes
Lawmakers
Judges (as Lawmakers)
Specific Case
Make a Prediction
Legal Outcome
LJP Keystone: Based on "Laws" by Courts/Judges
Figure 4: Legal Judgment Prediction (LJP) – Predictions Keystones
Source Author: Dr. Lance B. Eliot
V1.3

Figure 27

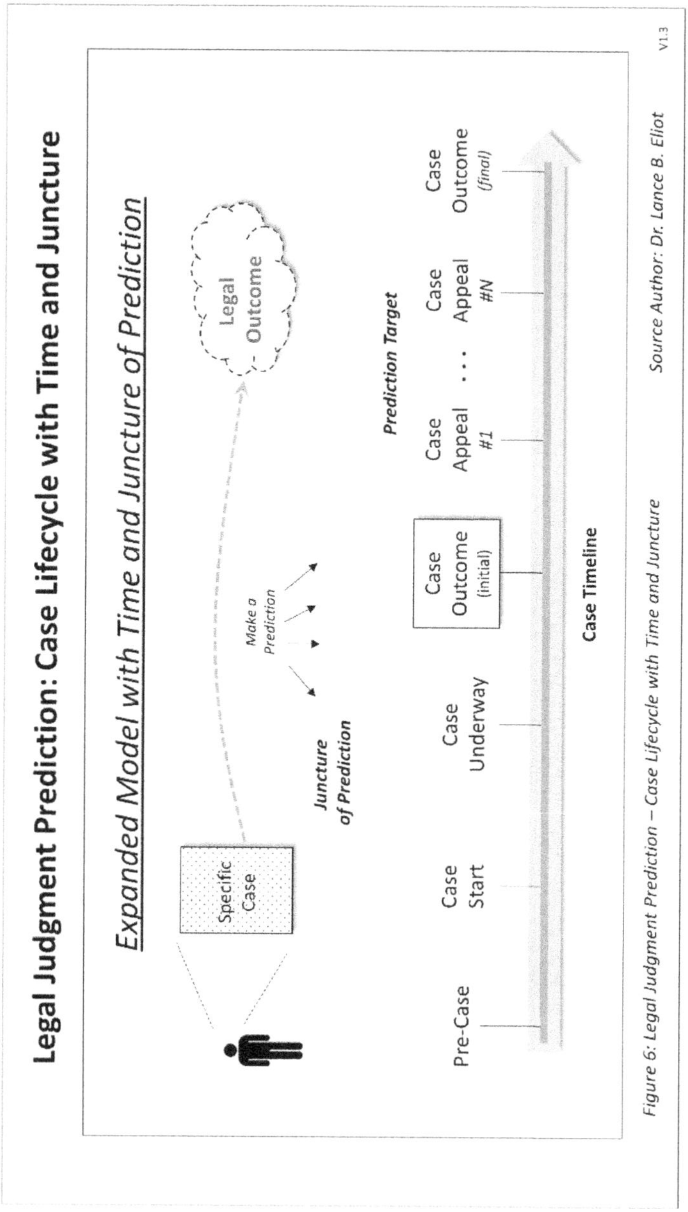
Legal Judgment Prediction: Case Lifecycle with Time and Juncture
Expanded Model with Time and Juncture of Prediction
Specific Case
Legal Outcome
Make a Prediction
Juncture of Prediction
Prediction Target
Pre-Case
Case Start
Case Underway
Case Outcome (initial)
Case Appeal #1
. . .
Case Appeal #N
Case Outcome (final)
Case Timeline
Figure 6: Legal Judgment Prediction – Case Lifecycle with Time and Juncture
Source Author: Dr. Lance B. Eliot
V1.3

Figure 28

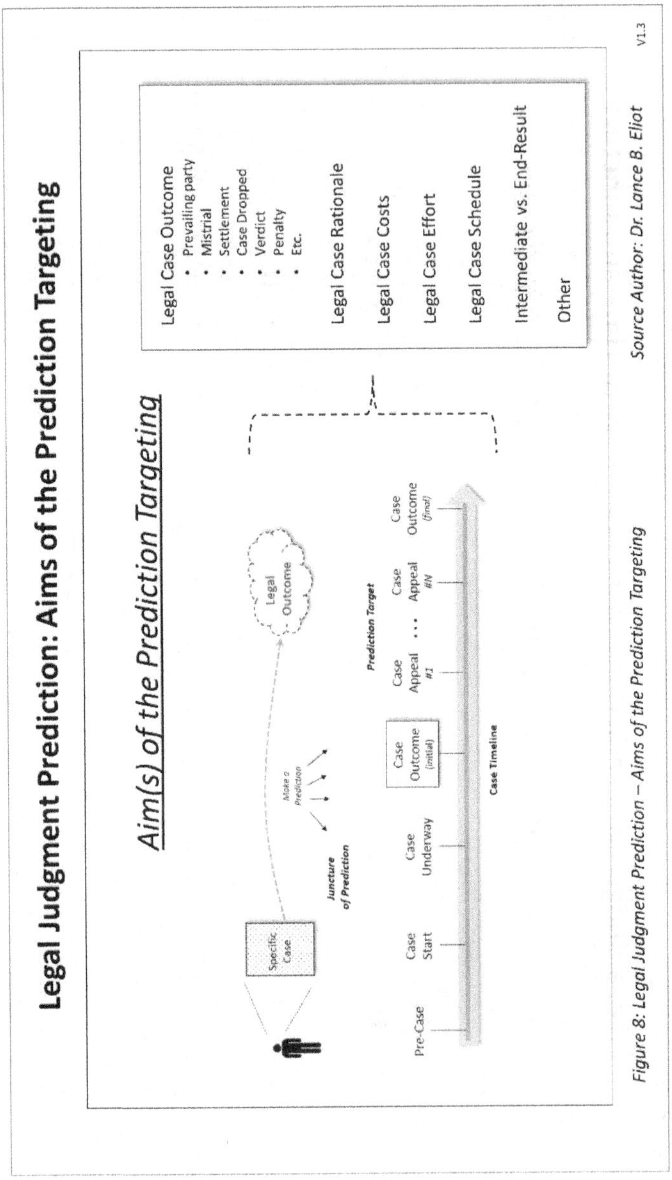
Legal Judgment Prediction: Aims of the Prediction Targeting
Aim(s) of the Prediction Targeting
Specific Case
Juncture of Prediction
Make a Prediction
Legal Outcome
Prediction Target
Pre-Case
Case Start
Case Underway
Case Outcome (initial)
Case Appeal #1
. . .
Case Appeal #N
Case Outcome (final)
Case Timeline
Legal Case Outcome
Prevailing party
Mistrial
Settlement
Case Dropped
Verdict
Penalty
Etc.
Legal Case Rationale
Legal Case Costs
Legal Case Effort
Legal Case Schedule
Intermediate vs. End-Result
Other
Figure 8: Legal Judgment Prediction – Aims of the Prediction Targeting
Source Author: Dr. Lance B. Eliot
V1.3

Figure 29

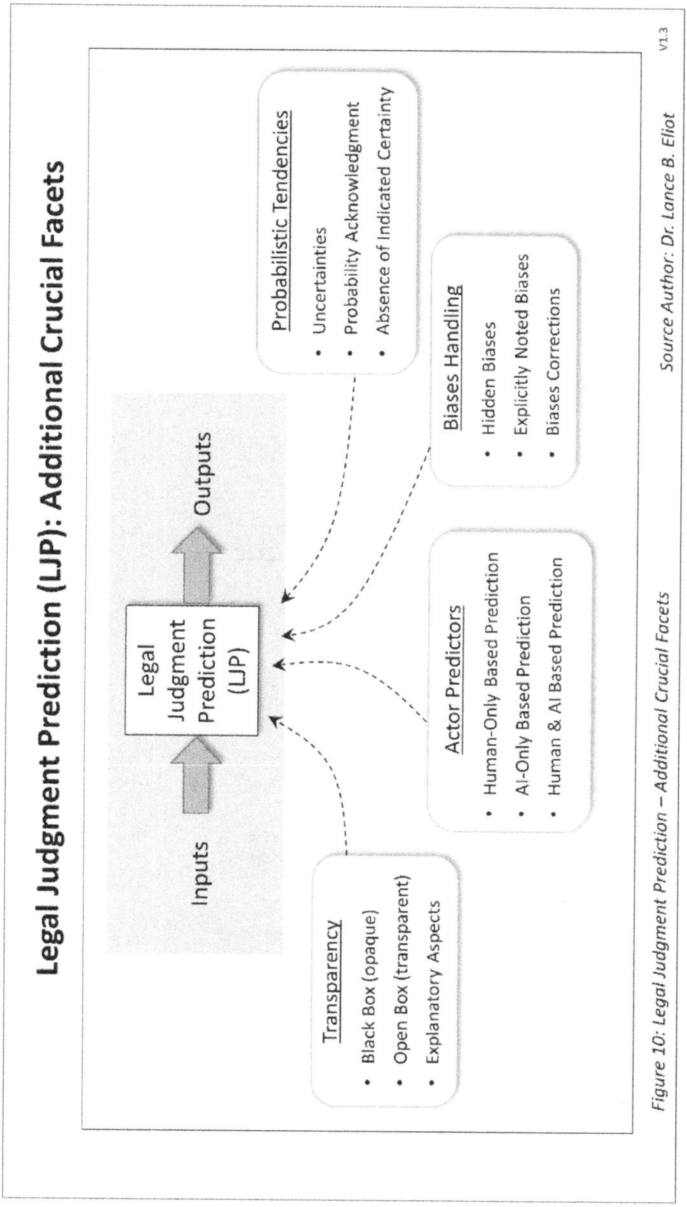
Legal Judgment Prediction (LJP): Additional Crucial Facets
Inputs
Legal Judgment Prediction (LJP)
Outputs
Transparency
Black Box (opaque)
Open Box (transparent)
Explanatory Aspects
Actor Predictors
Human-Only Based Prediction
AI-Only Based Prediction
Human & AI Based Prediction
Biases Handling
Hidden Biases
Explicitly Noted Biases
Biases Corrections
Probabilistic Tendencies
Uncertainties
Probability Acknowledgment
Absence of Indicated Certainty
Figure 10: Legal Judgment Prediction – Additional Crucial Facets
Source Author: Dr. Lance B. Eliot
V1.3

Figure 30

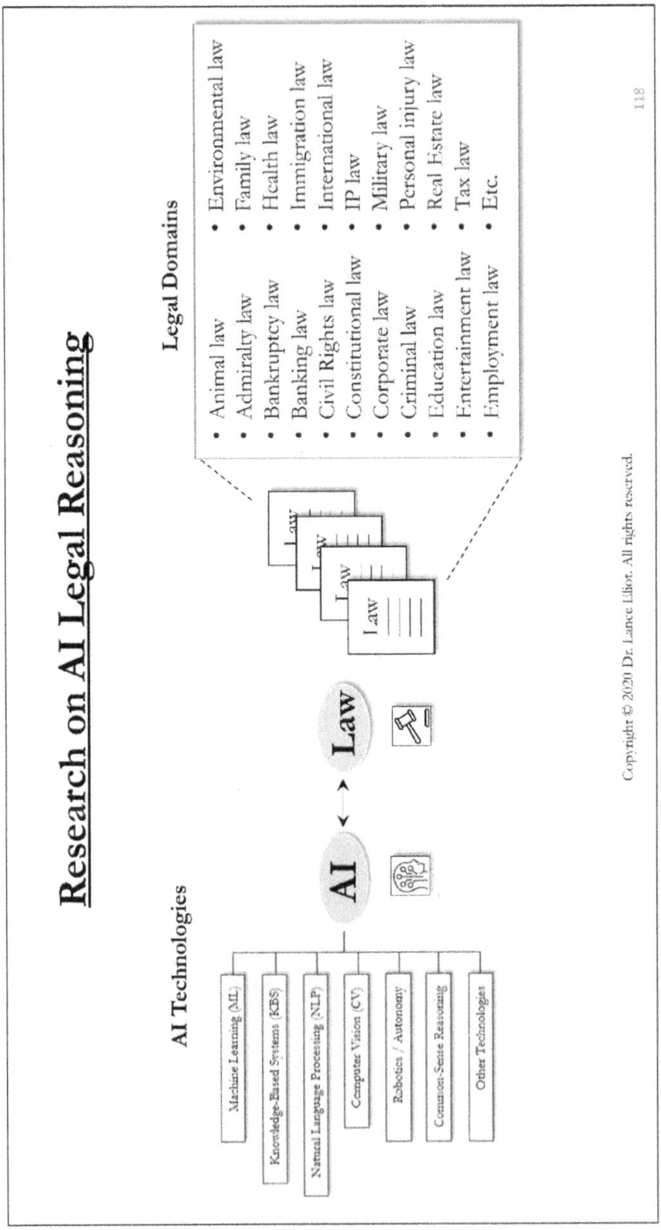
Research on AI Legal Reasoning
AI Technologies
Machine Learning (ML)
Knowledge-Based Systems (KBS)
Natural Language Processing (NLP)
Computer Vision (CV)
Robotics / Autonomy
Common-Sense Reasoning
Other Technologies
AI
Law
Law
Legal Domains
Animal law
Admiralty law
Bankruptcy law
Banking law
Civil Rights law
Constitutional law
Corporate law
Criminal law
Education law
Entertainment law
Employment law
Environmental law
Family law
Health law
Immigration law
International law
IP law
Military law
Personal injury law
Real Estate law
Tax law
Etc.
Copyright © 2020 Dr. Lance Eliot. All rights reserved.
118

Figure 31

ABOUT THE AUTHOR

Dr. Lance B. Eliot, Ph.D., MBA is a globally recognized AI expert and thought leader, an invited Stanford Fellow at Stanford University, an experienced top executive and corporate leader, a successful entrepreneur, and a noted scholar on AI, including that his Forbes and AI Trends columns have amassed over 4 million views, his books on AI are ranked in the Top 10 of all-time AI books, his journal articles are widely cited, and he has developed and implemented numerous AI systems.

He currently serves as the Chief AI Scientist at Techbruim, Inc. and has over twenty years of industry experience including serving as a corporate officer in billion-dollar sized firms and was a partner in a major consulting firm. He is also a successful entrepreneur having founded, ran, and sold several high-tech related businesses.

Dr. Eliot previously hosted the popular radio show *Technotrends* that was also available on American Airlines flights via their in-flight audio program, he has made appearances on CNN, has been a frequent speaker at industry conferences, and his podcasts have been downloaded over 150,000 times.

A former professor at the University of Southern California (USC), he founded and led an innovative research lab on Artificial Intelligence. He also previously served on the faculty of the University of California Los Angeles (UCLA) and was a visiting professor at other major universities. He was elected to the International Board of the Society for Information Management (SIM), a prestigious association of over 3,000 high-tech executives worldwide.

He has performed extensive community service, including serving as Senior Science Adviser to the Congressional Vice-Chair of the Congressional Committee on Science & Technology. He has served on the Board of the OC Science & Engineering Fair (OCSEF), where he is also has been a Grand Sweepstakes judge, and likewise served as a judge for the Intel International SEF (ISEF). He served as the Vice-Chair of the Association for Computing Machinery (ACM) Chapter, a prestigious association of computer scientists. Dr. Eliot has been a shark tank judge for the USC Mark Stevens Center for Innovation on start-up pitch competitions and served as a mentor for several incubators and accelerators in Silicon Valley and in Silicon Beach.

Dr. Eliot holds a Ph.D. from USC, MBA, and Bachelor's in Computer Science, and earned the CDP, CCP, CSP, CDE, and CISA certification.

Companion Book By Dr. Lance Eliot

"Artificial Intelligence and Legal Reasoning Essentials"

ISBN 978-1-73460165-7

Chapters

Companion Book By Dr. Lance Eliot

"Artificial Intelligence and LegalTech Essentials"

ISBN 978-1-7346016-3-3

Chapters

Available on Amazon and via other online book sellers

Companion Book By Dr. Lance Eliot

"Decisive Essays On AI And Law"

ISBN 978-1-73630310-8

Chapters

Available on Amazon and via other online book sellers

Companion Book By Dr. Lance Eliot

"Incisive Research On AI And Law"

ISBN 978-1-73630311-5

Chapters

Available on Amazon and via other online book sellers

Companion Book By Dr. Lance Eliot

"Ingenious Essays On AI And Law"

ISBN 978-1-73630312-2

Chapters

Available on Amazon and via other online book seller

Companion Book By Dr. Lance Eliot

"Compelling Essays On AI And Law"

ISBN 978-1-73630313-9

Chapters

Available on Amazon and via other online book sellers

Companion Book By Dr. Lance Eliot

"Topnotch Essays On AI And Law"

ISBN 978-1-73630314-6

Chapters

Available on Amazon and via other online book sellers

Companion Book By Dr. Lance Eliot

"Trendsetting Essays On AI And Law"

ISBN 978-1-95-738601-0

Chapters

Companion Book By Dr. Lance Eliot

"Pioneering Essays On AI And Law"

ISBN 978-1-95-738602-7

Chapters

ADDENDUM

Thanks for reading this book and I hope you will continue your interest in the field of AI & Law

---

For my free podcasts about AI & Law:

https://ai-law.libsyn.com/website

Those podcasts are also available on Spotify, iTunes, etc.

For the latest on AI & Law see my website:

www.ai-law.legal

To follow me on Twitter:

https://twitter.com/LanceEliot

For my in-depth book on AI & Law:

AI And Legal Reasoning Essentials

www.amazon.com/gp/product/1734601655/

Made in the USA
Monee, IL
05 November 2026

67808595R00125